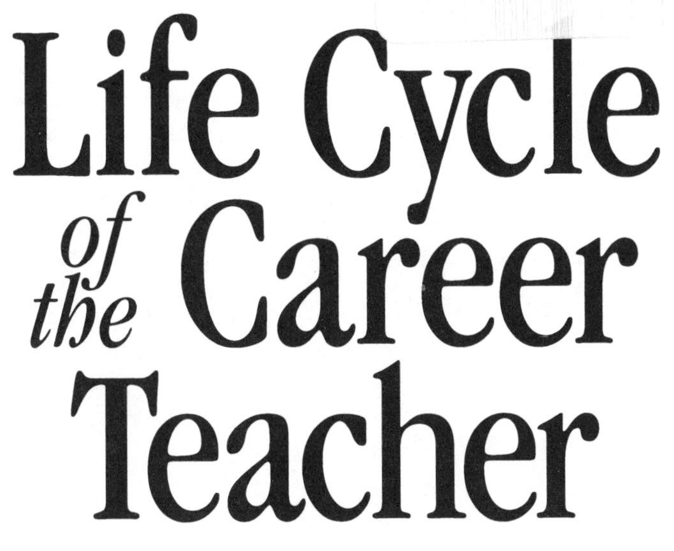

Life Cycle *of the* Career Teacher

Edited by Betty E. Steffy • Michael P. Wolfe
Suzanne H. Pasch • Billie J. Enz

A Joint Publication of

KAPPA DELTA PI,
International Honor Society
in Education

and

A joint publication of Kappa Delta Pi, International Honor Society in Education, and Corwin Press, Inc.

For information:

Corwin Press, Inc.
A Sage Publications Company
2455 Teller Road
Thousand Oaks, California 91320
E-mail: order@corwinpress.com

SAGE Publications Ltd.
6 Bonhill Street
London EC2A 4PU
United Kingdom

SAGE Publications India Pvt. Ltd.
M-32 Market
Greater Kailash I
New Delhi 110 048 India

Printed in the United States of America

Library of Congress Cataloging-in-Publication Data

Life cycle of the career teacher / edited by Betty E. Steffy . . . [et al.].
p. cm.
Includes bibliographical references and index.
ISBN 0-7619-7539-X (cloth)—ISBN 0-7619-7540-3 (paper)
1. Teachers—United States—Case studies. 2. Teachers—Training of—United States—Case studies. 3. Teachers—In-service training—United States—Case studies. I. Steffy, Betty E. II. Kappa Delta Pi (Honor society)

LB1775.2 .L54 2000
371.1'00973 21—dc21 99-046010

This book is printed on acid-free paper.

00 01 02 03 04 05 10 9 8 7 6 5 4 3 2 1

Contents

Foreword

To talk in public, to think in solitude, to read and to hear, to inquire and answer inquiries, is the business of the scholar.

Samuel Johnson (1709–84)
The History of Rasselas, Prince of Abissinia

All contributors to this book are career teachers who care deeply about the growth of young students. All are teacher educators and scholars who care about the preparation and continuing professional development of teachers. *Life Cycle of the Career Teacher* represents the collaborative effort of several members of Kappa Delta Pi, International Honor Society in Education, who share the belief that all students deserve only the best teachers.

Powerful forces are affecting the education profession. The teaching workforce must grow dramatically to meet current and projected increases in student enrollment. Simultaneously, the attrition rate among teachers is escalating due to retirements and new-teacher dropouts. Thus, the supply cannot meet demands. Other factors like declining test scores, school violence, vouchers, and inadequate funding contribute to the seemingly overwhelming challenges facing educators.

Along with defining the life cycle of the career teacher, this book consitutes a call for action. We believe that all students should have access to competent, caring, and qualified teachers in schools organized for success.

Underscoring the importance of the teacher in the learning process, this collection of chapters supports the idea that what teachers know and can do is the most important influence on what students can learn. We believe that the quality of teachers is a major factor in determining the quality of schools. Paying direct attention to ongoing teacher development is the key to maintaining quality in our profession.

The Life Cycle of the Career Teacher model crosses the continuum of practice from preservice preparation through professional development. It encompasses the lives of classroom teachers, from the time they engage in their first practicum experiences to beyond the time they retire. Spanning more than 50 years of a teacher's career, this model can ensure that all students interact with expert teachers—a label now reserved for only a few. Our model purports that all new teachers can reach this standard within the first 5 years of teaching and maintain it for a lifetime—if they continue to develop as professionals.

Do we have a choice? Students deserve our best.

Michael P. Wolfe
Executive Director, Kappa Delta Pi

Acknowledgments

Life Cycle of the Career Teacher is a book about maintaining excellence for a lifetime of teaching. This project became a labor of love for a group of dedicated and passionate teachers and teacher educators. Four editors worked with 18 authors and three contributors for a year. The authors—all members of Kappa Delta Pi, International Honor Society in Education—are listed elsewhere in the book and represent a diverse group of educators; their contributions have made this book a reality. Three educators—Dr. Gary DeBolt, Assistant Superintendent, Fairport, New York; Dr. John Maddaus, Associate Professor of Education, University of Maine; and Dr. Fenwick W. English, Professor of Educational Administration, Iowa State University—provided early insights and feedback that helped shape the book. In addition, members of the National State Teachers of the Year contributed experiences that enhanced the chapter on the Distinguished Teacher.

The Kappa Delta Pi Publications Department, including Grant E. Mabie, Nicholas Drake, and Karen Allen, provided expert editing prowess and feedback resulting in a consistent style of content and format. We are indebted to Karen Klutzke, art director, Kappa Delta Pi, for creative layout and design of the text. Margo Black, administrative assistant, provided production assistance and support during the final stages of writing.

A final acknowledgment goes to Corwin Press for its role in the final editing, production, and distribution of the book. We hope that this first collaborative venture between Kappa Delta Pi and Corwin Press sets a positive tone for future projects.

It is time for *Life Cycle of the Career Teacher* to be shared widely with a profession in search of recognition for making a positive difference in people's lives. This book will inform the conversation that must occur for teaching to be a career-long commitment to reflection, renewal, and growth. Everyone knows that a teacher can affect eternity, and we want this impact to be positive. Every classroom needs a competent, caring, and qualified teacher. The individuals who have contributed to this project believe in this goal, and we are grateful for their efforts.

Betty E. Steffy
Michael P. Wolfe
Suzanne H. Pasch
Billie J. Enz

About the Authors

Michael J. Berson is an Assistant Professor of Social Science Education in the Department of Secondary Education at the University of South Florida. His research explores technology in social studies education, the use of primary source materials in instruction, and global child advocacy.

Jane S. Bray is an Associate Professor and Chairperson of the Department of Early Childhood and Elementary Education at East Stroudsburg University in Pennsylvania. She teaches undergraduate and graduate courses in elementary education. Her research interests include student teaching, student teachers, cooperating teachers, and the stages of development for new teachers.

Rick A. Breault is an Associate Professor of Education in the Department of Teacher Education at the University of Indianapolis. He teaches courses in social foundations and curriculum development and supervises student teachers. His research interests include preservice teacher thinking and the role of school-university partnerships in new teacher induction.

Ruth D. Campopiano is a retired teacher / administrator from the West Morris Region High School District in Chester, New Jersey. She taught world languages and was 1975 New Jersey Teacher of the Year. Her current interests include mentoring and recruitment of new teachers through Kappa Delta Pi's Celebration of Teaching program.

Mary C. Clement is an Assistant Professor of Education at Berry College in Mt. Berry, Georgia. She teaches introduction to education, middle and secondary methods, foreign language methods, and graduate curriculum courses. Her research interests include the hiring and induction of new teachers, as well as classroom management for student teachers.

Raymond J. Dagenais is the Science Curriculum and Assessment Leader and a physics teacher at the Illinois Mathematics and Science Academy. His research focus includes investigating characteristics of successful mentoring experiences and standards for successful mentoring programs.

Billie J. Enz is the Professional Director of Initial Teacher Certification and Induction in the College of Education at Arizona State University–Main. Her interests include teacher preparation and language and literacy development.

Pamela A. Kramer is an Associate Professor of Education at East Stroudsburg University in Pennsylvania. She teaches undergraduate and graduate courses in early childhood and elementary education. Her research interests include teacher induction, professionalism, and bibliotherapy.

Denise LePage is an Associate Professor of Education at East Stroudsburg University in Pennsylvania. She teaches undergraduate and graduate courses in mathematics, curriculum development, and educational technology. Her professional areas of interest primarily focus on the integration of technology in education.

Vincent R. McGrath is a Professor of Education at Mississippi State University. He teaches foundations of education and comparative education. His research interests include philosophy of science, logical inquiry, and critical-thinking skills.

Diane S. Murphy is an Associate Professor of Teacher Education in the School of Education at Seattle University. Her research explores beginning-teacher support programs, assessment of student learning in relation to teacher performance, and multiculturalism.

Suzanne H. Pasch is Dean of Education and Graduate Studies and a Professor of Education at The College of New Jersey, where she is also responsible for administration and oversight of all international programs. She has a particular interest in urban and global education.

George E. Pawlas is an Associate Professor of Educational Leadership at the University of Central Florida in Orlando. His research interests include teacher and administrator preparation, rural education, and home schooling.

Patricia H. Phelps is an Associate Professor of Administration and Secondary Education at the University of Central Arkansas in Conway. She teaches secondary education, classroom management, and graduate instruction courses. Her research interests include parent-teacher collaboration, new teacher induction and classroom management.

Betty E. Steffy is a Professor of Educational Administration in the College of Education at Iowa State University. She is coauthor of five books and is the cofounder and coeditor of the academic peer-reviewed quarterly, *The International Journal of Educational Reform.* Her research interests include new-teacher induction, school reform, and administrator preparation.

Kathleen R. Weber is a primary teacher at Nelson School in Edwardsville, Illinois. She teaches second grade and was the 1984 Illinois Teacher of the Year and a 1996 Milken National Educator award recipient. Her current interests include puppetry, creative learning, and teacher development.

Michael P. Wolfe is the Executive Director of Kappa Delta Pi, International Honor Society in Education. He is a former university professor and administrator in teacher education and has authored numerous journal articles and books. His research interests include school reform, creating a positive school climate, enhancing self-concept, and teacher-induction practices.

Polly Wolfe is an Assistant Professor of Art Education at The Herron School of Art, Indiana University–Purdue University at Indianapolis. Her research centers on curriculum-development processes by master teachers and teaching and learning in the artistically gifted classroom.

The Model and Its Application 1

by Betty E. Steffy, Michael P. Wolfe, Suzanne H. Pasch, and Billie J. Enz

Daily News, Anytown, USA

Wanted: Competent, Caring, and Qualified Teacher

Student focused, passionate professional, committed to learning, and well versed in subject-area content. Understands human development and learning, thrives on chaos, avoids burnout and withdrawal by remaining engaged in own learning. Leads successfully in technological milieu, arbitrates disputes, and juggles multiple tasks. Simultaneously relates well and works collaboratively with colleagues, parents, the business community, service organizations, church groups, administrators, students, social service agencies, and others. Candidates should be knowledgeable and skilled in generating research-based teaching and learning strategies, including, but not limited to, cooperative learning, multicultural emphases, developmentally appropriate practices, school-to-work initiatives, service learning, brain-based learning, multiple intelligences, conflict resolution, and parental involvement. Master's degree and minimum of one year professional or mentored experience required. Commitment to lifelong continual professional development mandatory.

A considerable body of literature exists on the nature of the teaching environment and its effect on teaching practice (Haberman, 1995; Lortie, 1975), on the nature and practice of reflection (Schön, 1983; Zeichner, Tabachnik, & Densmore, 1987), on the relationship between adult development and teaching (Levine, 1989), and on the professional development of teachers (Huberman, Grounauer, & Marti, 1993). There are, however, few comprehensive attempts to put it all together in a systematic way that both characterizes and encourages lifelong career-teacher development. That is the intent of this book.

As we synthesize a number of influences on teacher development, we propose a direction and a continuum of phases that describe teacher development. Though further research is needed to confirm the phases in the Life Cycle of the Career Teacher model, we present movement through these phases as a means for teachers to stay vital, informed, and purposeful over time and, as a result, maintain excellence across a lifetime of teaching for the benefit of all learners.

Promoting a Vision of Teaching for a Lifetime of Practice

We believe that teachers who spend their careers in classrooms have the capacity to maintain excellence for a lifetime. The Life Cycle of the Career Teacher model is based in the belief that all teachers can reach a standard of excellence within the first 5 years of teaching and, with the appropriate support, continue to enhance their abilities throughout their careers. This model is grounded in literature on teaching, learning, schooling, and classroom practice. Though drawn from and intended for educators in the United States, this model also has universal applications.

The Life Cycle of the Career Teacher model is both descriptive and prescriptive. It describes a progression of developmental phases and the positive growth that results when teachers strive for, achieve, and maintain a standard of excellence that provides all children with competent, caring, and qualified teachers. It also prescribes for each phase the enrichment of the profession that results from providing teachers with the support they deserve. Some professional-development efforts have been characterized as offering too little and too late or too much and too soon. To this end, our model recommends appropriate strategies and approaches to ensure sufficient support occurs at each phase and in a manner that encourages continued development.

The phases are progressive and influenced by a variety of factors, such as individual development and social context. Consistent with a constructivist view of learning, however, the most significant mechanism impelling growth in this model is choice (Yager, 1991). Teachers make choices that help them grow or cause them to withdraw. The ongoing process of reflection and renewal propels teacher growth. Conversely, the absence of reflection and renewal leads to disengagement or withdrawal.

This model is not value neutral. Implicit in the Life Cycle of the Career Teacher model are several basic assumptions grounded in research, theory, and best practices about the nature of teaching and teachers. These assumptions include the following:

- Teacher development is directional and impelled by the need to improve.
- The level of development in the life cycle of teaching is a function of personal characteristics, school contexts, support systems, and solid preparation.
- A community of inquiry about teaching encourages learning among teachers and students.
- Teaching excellence is influenced by one's ability to learn, do scholarly work, and commit to growth.
- Situation or context is a powerful force for growth and / or withdrawal.
- Excellence in teaching depends upon the centrality of caring—for students, self, ideas, and the profession.

The Life Cycle of the Career Teacher

The Life Cycle of the Career Teacher is an advocacy model. It describes teacher development and offers a prescription for enhancing the teaching profession. We advocate that teachers *must* develop through progressive phases to sustain a career-long standard of excellence. Attention *must* be paid to encouraging the process of reflection and renewal that leads to growth at each phase. Furthermore, the progression of phases and the reflection-renewal-growth process that underlies each phase *will* put the vision of teaching into operation—but only to the extent that teachers, administrators, teacher educators, and researchers work together to make this vision a reality.

The Life Cycle of the Career Teacher model constitutes a vision of teaching that can (1) bridge preservice and in-service teacher education; (2) create a viable platform to provide professional-growth opportunities for classroom teachers throughout their lifetime; and (3) enable all teachers to attain the status of—and be recognized as—competent, caring, and qualified professionals. Such growth does not occur automatically or in a vacuum. If we are to deliver on the promise to provide all students with competent, caring, and qualified teachers capable of facilitating learning in all environments, we must individually exercise the will and collaborative interaction to put this model into practice.

For as long as teaching as an art or science has been studied, writers and researchers have conceptualized and studied phases of development in the teacher career (Fuller, 1969; Gehrke, 1987; Huberman et al., 1993; Katz, 1977; VanderVen, 1988). Most of the work posits development on a continuum from novice to expert. Little attention has been paid to the nature of the intermittent steps between inexperience and expertise, factors and processes that influence teacher growth over time, and those that allow for reflection about teaching. Our life-cycle model addresses these issues by providing a framework for supporting career-long professional development at each phase.

Phases or Stages?

The Life Cycle of the Career Teacher is a *developmental* model that consists of six progressive phases propelled by the mechanisms of reflection and renewal or impeded by withdrawal (Steffy & Wolfe, 1997). The model is developmental because it proposes and describes an ongoing process that takes place throughout a life cycle—in this instance, the life cycle of a teaching career. In common with other developmental theories, the model views growth as unfolding through interactions between persons and their environments in an identifiable, sequential pattern; acknowledges that individuals move along the continuum at different rates; and views the growing individual as an active participant in his or her own development.

The model posits phases of development in common with Erikson (1968); Levinson, Darrow, Klein, Levinson, & McKee (1978); and others. *Phase theories* tend to focus on content and tasks that flow from one to another along a continuum. In contrast, *stage theories*, such as those

Figure 1.1. Phases of Teacher Growth
Reprinted by permission from Betty E. Steffy and Michael P. Wolfe, *The Life Cycle of the Career Teacher: Maintaining Excellence for a Lifetime*, p. 5. © 1997, Kappa Delta Pi, an International Honor Society in Education.

of Piaget (1954), Loevinger (1987), and others, focus more on structure and organization and typically are more discrete in their relationships to one another. In the Life Cycle of the Career Teacher model, each of the six phases is content and task specific and exists along the continuum of excellent teaching across the career.

Life-Cycle Phases of the Career Teacher

Through review of the literature and systematic observation of teachers over time, we have identified six basic phases—as shown in Figure 1.1 above—that committed classroom teachers experience during their careers: novice, apprentice, professional, expert, distinguished, and emeritus (Steffy & Wolfe, 1997). Teachers take this path in developing and maintaining professional growth.

The Life Cycle of the Career Teacher model offers a developmental continuum useful for promoting efficacy as a teacher. It presents a vision of good practice based on transferring knowledge and contextual experience to another phase. Thus, the lines are blurred between the life-cycle phases of a career teacher. The strength of this model is its focus on the process of how one continues to grow and become a more competent career teacher along the continuum.

Novice Teacher

The *novice* phase begins when preservice students first encounter practicum experiences as part of their teacher education program and continues through student teaching and the intern experience. In some universities and colleges, preservice teachers enter this phase during the freshman year. For others, these field experiences may not begin until the junior year. For fifth-year programs, students enter the novice cycle at the graduate level.

Novice teachers begin to acquire the skills necessary to function effectively in the classroom. Preparation in liberal arts, specific subject matter, and a professional and pedagogical course sequence begin. Because they have not mastered the skills of the profession or the learning content, most preservice teachers are hesitant and unsure of themselves. As they visit classrooms, they are often amazed at the master teacher's skill at arranging classroom activities. Some are uncertain they will ever be able to direct the learning activities of all those energetic students.

In time, novice teachers acquire more skills. They begin to see how teachers create a learning environment. Their confidence grows as they succeed with students and learn more about themselves and classroom practices. They become sensitive to the needs of children and slowly acquire the skills to be competent teachers. As they grow in skill and self-confidence, novices reflect on newly acquired skills and experiences, then enter the apprentice phase.

Apprentice Teacher

The *apprentice* phase begins for most teachers when they receive responsibility for planning and delivering instruction on their own. This phase continues until integration and synthesis of knowledge, pedagogy, and confidence emerges, marking the beginning of the professional period. Typically, the apprentice phase includes the induction period and extends into the second or third year of teaching.

Teachers at this career phase are filled with energy and anticipation. Following all the professional-preparation courses and field experiences, they are able to stand before a group of students and be called "teacher." Notwithstanding feelings of self-doubt, many love teaching and believe they have the skills to assure that *all* children will achieve at high levels.

Apprentice teachers tend to be idealistic. They believe they have the ability and drive necessary to motivate all children. Apprentice teachers are open to new ideas. They tend to volunteer to serve on committees or work on extracurricular activities. They are creative and growth oriented. They want to learn more and are willing to try new strategies. No child is too difficult in their eyes. No parent seems unwilling to support a child's learning. Though teachers at the apprentice phase may yet be unsure of their skills, they are passionate about helping students succeed. Still, they must learn how to achieve their high ideals.

Unfortunately, about one third of all newly hired teachers leave the field within the first few years of teaching (National Commission on Teaching and America's Future [NCTAF], 1996). This form of withdrawal is a waste of a valuable resource. For many of these teachers, leaving is not so much related to a lack of skill as it is to a perceived lack of efficacy in the role of teacher. Overwhelmed with the demands of their profession, enthusiastic apprentice teachers may become disillusioned. With proper encouragement and appropriate support, however, most of these teachers can maintain the ideals of the apprentice. If they avoid withdrawal and continue to reflect critically on their experiences, renewal and growth can lead them to the next phase in their careers.

Professional Teacher

The *professional* phase emerges as teachers grow in their self-confidence as educators. Student feedback plays a critical role in this process. Students' respect for teachers and teachers' respect for students form the bedrock foundation upon which this stage is built. Students view professional teachers as patient, kind, understanding, and helpful. In turn, these teachers view themselves as student advocates.

Most school faculties are composed of large numbers of professional teachers. They form the backbone of the profession. They are competent, solid, and dependable. Most view themselves as classroom teachers with no aspirations to become administrators. These teachers are happiest when interacting with students. Their greatest reward comes from the positive regard students provide—present and past. Without exception, they cherish notes from students describing how their lives have been changed by the teacher.

Because professional teachers look to their students to provide them with motivation, administrators often treat them differently, give them less attention, and take them for granted. Administrators must be especially careful to acknowledge the valuable contribution teachers at the professional phase make to the effective functioning of the school.

Professional teachers most frequently seek help and assistance from other teachers. They actively participate in a collegial network for support and guidance. They begin to look beyond the classroom, seeing themselves and their colleagues as part of a broader profession. These teachers have satisfied the requirements for state licensing and regularly use a variety of professional-development opportunities for continued growth.

Professional teachers value opportunities to observe colleagues' innovative practices. They know that finding time for reflection is a luxury in most school environments. However, they also realize that continued growth and development depends on ample opportunities for observation, reflection, and interaction.

Expert Teacher

The *expert* phase symbolizes achievement of the high standards desired by the NCTAF (1996). Even if they do not formally seek it, these teachers meet the expectations required for national certification (Steffy 1989). The premise of the Life Cycle of the Career Teacher model is to assure that all teachers develop their skills to operate at this expert level.

Expert teachers anticipate student responses, modifying and adjusting instruction to promote growth. Teachers at this level competently support, facilitate, and nurture growth and development of all students, regardless of their backgrounds or ability levels. Students feel safe in the environment of mutual respect these teachers create.

Teachers in this phase can be described as being "with it." Thus, students know what is expected of them, and most behave accordingly. These teachers are in tune with the learning styles, needs, and interests of their students, who likewise are in tune with their teachers.

Expert teachers are able to reflect on their practice, facilitating growth and change. They are committed to the newest and best ideas in the profession. They are usually connected with other expert teachers within the district, region, and state. They hold leadership roles in professional associations and content-area organizations, taking great pride in maintaining cutting-edge expertise.

Expert teachers learn through their roles as teachers and community leaders. They embody what parents and society desire for unlocking the learning of children. These teachers understand that students are inclined to learn. In the absence of serious obstacles, this phase can last for the lifetime of a teacher.

Distinguished Teacher

The *distinguished* phase is reserved for teachers truly gifted in their field. They exceed current expectations for what teachers are expected to know and do. These teachers are the "pied pipers" of the profession. Students, parents, administrators, and the community revere them. The potential roster of distinguished teachers is limited to those who achieve the expert phase.

Distinguished teachers impact education-related decisions at city, state, and national levels. Indeed, policymakers and lawmakers at all levels regularly consult distinguished teacher groups, including the National State Teachers of the Year, the Milkin Teacher Award recipients, and the Golden Apple Fellows.

Distinguished teachers bring to their schools a richer, wider education experience. Through the application of this model, we believe that the number of distinguished teachers will increase as schools reduce the number of potential distinguished teachers who leave the field at the apprentice level or who have entered withdrawal.

Emeritus Teacher

The *emeritus* phase marks a lifetime of achievement in education. For some teachers, leaving their career is an end; for others, it marks a new beginning. Following retirement from classroom teaching, many career educators choose to honor their lifelong commitment to students by continuing to serve the profession in alternative roles. Some move into administrative positions; others pursue new beginnings in higher education. Preparing for this involvement begins prior to leaving the classroom.

Teachers who retire after a lifetime of teaching deserve society's recognition and praise. They have served tirelessly, often under difficult conditions. These teachers leave their profession feeling satisfied by the legacy they leave behind: thousands of students whose lives have been forever enriched by a quality education.

As life expectancy increases due to better health care, good physical fitness programs, and sound nutritional practices, more teachers can remain active educators for longer periods of time. Furthermore, educators operating at expert and distinguished levels tend to remain more active than those who experience withdrawal prior to exiting the profession.

A select few retired educators remain so active in the field that they earn emeritus status. These teachers have formally retired but, because of their expertise and devotion, continue to contribute to the profession. The transition to emeritus status involves identifying new ways to serve others. Through consultation, volunteerism, mentoring, and service activities with professional groups, these teachers are strong advocates and lobbyists for teachers.

Emeritus teachers may use their skills and experience to consult with teacher education programs, serving as supervisors for novice or apprentice teachers as well as coteaching pedagogy courses. Many volunteer time and energy to promote literacy programs, tutoring sessions, school clean-up campaigns, and playground construction projects. Various types of mentoring projects have been initiated using emeritus educators' skills in assisting students, new teachers, administrators, and parents. Community action programs can be initiated that positively support schools' missions as well.

The activities of emeriti who continue to contribute to the profession in retirement are worthy of our notice. Indeed, we must support the work of these teachers. Creating feelings of self-worth and promoting a useful and active retirement results in gains for everyone—the students, the schools, the systems, the administrators, and, of course, the exiting teachers.

Reflection and Renewal: The Mechanism of Growth

The process of reflection and renewal is the central, critical aspect of our model. It relates thought and action. It connects present knowledge and skills to a vision for a desired future. From this vision, teachers construct strategies that enable them to effectuate their develop-

Figure 1.2. Reflection-Renewal-Growth Cycle Model
Reprinted by permission from Betty E. Steffy and Michael P. Wolfe, *The Life Cycle of the Career Teacher: Maintaining Excellence for a Lifetime*, p. 5. © 1997, Kappa Delta Pi, an International Honor Society in Education.

ment. Through this process, growth occurs.

As Bell and Gilbert (1996, p. 67) note, "Reflection is a skill which is inherently part of constructivism, particularly personal constructivism." Reflection must be purposeful, wherein teachers construct meaning and knowledge for themselves. How we change over time involves the interchange between personal and social contexts, which can be positive or negative. These interchanges create a continual tension for teachers moving through the life cycle. The positive forces are depicted in the Reflection-Renewal-Growth Cycle Model as shown in Figure 1.2 above.

Dewey (1910, p. 12) described reflective thinking as a process of hesitation or a state of doubt that leads to "the act of searching, hunting, inquiring to find material that will resolve the doubt, settle and dispose of the perplexity." Thus, the teacher as thinker is thrown into a state of cognitive dissonance. Through thoughtful reflection and acquisition of new knowledge, the thinker develops alternative ways of resolving doubt. With the doubt resolved, a feeling of renewal and growth manifests.

Dewey believed that resolving the cognitive dissonance involved five phases of reflective thought: suggestions, problems, hypothesis, reasoning, and testing. Building on these ideas, Schön (1983, 1987) posited that, in the practice of teaching, individuals display knowledge-in-action, reflection-in-action, and reflection-on-action. Knowledge-in-action relates to the ability to synthesize knowledge with activity. This process is seamless. What we know informs our actions, consciously. Reflection-in-action involves analysis, judgment, and action as we teach. Grimmett and Erickson (1988) described this process as being perplexed by a teaching situation, relating the present situation to one addressed in the past, reframing the solution, and applying it. Reflection-on-action takes place after the event. It can involve seeking new knowledge and a change in dispositions.

Among other researchers who looked at Schön's work on reflection, Zeichner, Tabachnik, and Densmore (1987), as well as Zeichner (1994), have identified three strategies that relate to personal reflection and one that relates to a social view of learning and critical inquiry. The first three applications concern reflection about subject matter, pedagogy, and student needs. The fourth stresses reflection about the context in which learning takes place and the social and political forces shaping that context.

The process of growth presented in the Life Cycle of the Career Teacher model is based on the assumption that reflection includes acquiring new knowledge and focuses on reflection-on-practice. Reflective notes, case studies, journals, and diaries are all "modalities" for reflection. These materials can be combined with research articles, books, and monographs to promote growth. Use of these materials in effective reflection requires a "commitment to and valuing of the writing and thinking necessary" to engage in the process (Loughran, 1996, p. 8). The reflective teacher may acquire new knowledge through dialogue with colleagues, conference attendance, and organized professional-development activities. For this new knowledge to be internalized and to impact practice, the teacher often needs the assistance of a coach. The development of the reflective practitioner may involve a skilled tutor (Bell & Gilbert, 1996).

As Osterman and Kottkamp (1993, p. 43) state, "Reflective practice, like an orchid, requires special conditions to thrive. One of the most important elements in the environment is trust." Osterman and Kottkamp developed a "credo for reflective practice" that includes the following key assumptions: (1) everyone needs professional-growth opportunities; (2) all professionals want to improve; (3) all professionals can learn; (4) all professionals are capable of assuming responsibility for their own professional growth and development; (5) people need and want information about their own performance; and (6) collaboration enriches professional development.

Boud, Keogh, and Walker (1985, p. 19) noted the periodical nature of reflection: "The capacity to reflect is developed to different stages in different people, and it may be this ability which characterizes those who learn effectively from experience." Furthermore, Dewey (1910) identified three attitudes necessary for a person to engage in successful reflection: open-mindedness, whole-heartedness, and responsibility. Open-mindedness means that the learner is willing to acknowledge a problem may exist, remains open to exploring options to solve it, and explores alternative solutions that may challenge his or her basic belief system. Whole-heartedness means there is commitment and enthusiasm to finding a solution. Responsibility means accepting ownership for being part of the problem and finding a solution. It is both a moral trait and an intellectual resource.

The Process of Renewal: How Reflection Supports Growth

To maintain professional growth, teachers must continually experience or initiate a process of reflection and renewal. Reflection and renewal propel teachers through the different phases of their career. Thus, novice teachers become apprentices by acquiring craft knowledge and internalizing meaning derived from reflection about their skills and general knowledge. Educators move from one phase to another through reflection, renewal, and growth. Literature on reflective practice supports the notion that continued professional growth occurs through this process (Valli, 1997).

Reflective practice can be a powerful mechanism for change. Osterman and Kottkamp (1993, p. 19) describe reflection "as a means by which practitioners can develop a greater level of self-awareness about the nature and impact of their performance." For teachers, the process is based on thinking about the results of the work they and other teachers do in classrooms. Lessons are planned and taught. The anticipated outcome is that students will learn; in most classes, however, some students do not learn. There is an increasing number of students for whom instructional approaches used in the classroom do not lead to the acquisition of intended learning.

Most teachers reflect on both their successes and failures with students. Teachers decide to change through this reflective process. Indeed, change *only* happens when teachers accept responsibility for students' learning. If teachers believe that a lack of learning is due to faults inherent in students, their families, or society, there will be little or no change in teacher behavior. When teachers accept responsibility for student learning, they are inclined to reflect on each teaching moment and any improvements needed to increase learning. Teachers grow when they feel in control of student learning. If teachers do not feel effective, then they have little confidence in their ability to increase student learning.

Reflective teachers constantly replay the events of teaching moments in their minds. In addition, they continually observe students to become more conscious of their teaching practices and their impact. Through the process of reflection, teachers analyze their lessons and remain open to alternative possibilities, asking, "What if I do this? What if I alter the material in this way?" Reflective teachers imagine how students will respond to different and new teaching methods.

As teachers reconceptualize lessons, they invariably create alternative strategies that may be more successful. They design new experiences for children. Thus, the change process evolves.

The reflection-and-renewal process propels teachers' growth through the phases of their career. Through this introspection, teachers grow and renew themselves as career educators. Reflection helps teachers identify areas of self-improvement. Once these areas are identified, a period of reactivated growth ensues. This new learning focuses on specific skills, perfecting new instructional strategies or embellishing skills already in the teacher's repertoire. Of course, this growth may also lead to changes in beliefs and attitudes. In all the career phases, teachers may experience the reflection-renewal-growth process. Sometimes enrollment in continuing education courses brings about change. Other teachers simply rely on self-initiative. In most cases, these teachers turn to colleagues and administrators for support.

Teachers do not have the luxury of developing new skills in a virtual-reality classroom. They practice and perfect their skills in real classrooms and with the students assigned to them. It takes a strong teacher to say to a class, "I am going to try something new today, and I want you to be my critics to help me improve." Yet that is what we ask of our students every day. We ask them to stretch and acquire new ways of learning. If we are serious about creating a learning community, then everyone in that community—teachers, administrators, and students alike—should be engaged in the reflection-renewal-growth process.

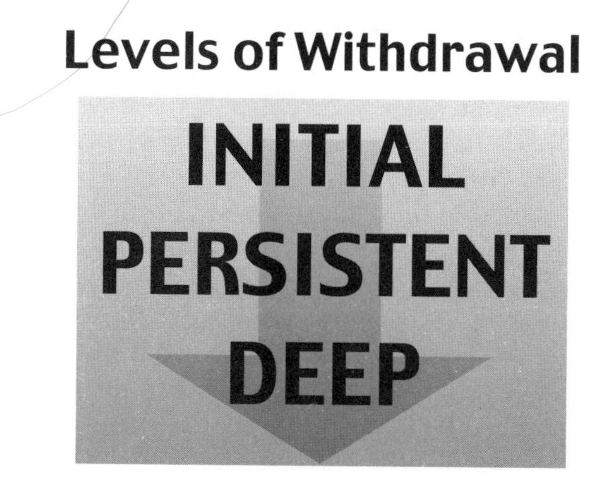

Figure 1.3. Levels of Withdrawal
Reprinted by permission from Betty E. Steffy and Michael P. Wolfe, *The Life Cycle of the Career Teacher: Maintaining Excellence for a Lifetime*, p. 8. © 1997, Kappa Delta Pi, an International Honor Society in Education.

Withdrawal: How Growth Is Constrained

Withdrawal is a form of disengagement. It represents the negative forces that cause educators to remove themselves psychologically from the reflection-renewal-growth process. Steffy (1989) identified three levels of withdrawal: initial, persistent, and deep. Left unattended, an educator who begins the downward slide into initial withdrawal can become a detriment to students, schools, and our profession (Steffy & Wolfe, 1997), as illustrated in Figure 1.3 above.

The progression from initial to persistent to deep withdrawal features increasingly negative teacher characteristics in three key areas: physical, emotional, and mental (Pines, Aronson, & Kafrey, 1981). Physical characteristics include low energy, chronic fatigue, weakness, and weariness. There may be an increase in the number of illnesses contracted and accidents experienced. Other physical signals include the use of chemicals or alcohol and evidence of eating disorders. Emotional signals of withdrawal include depression, helplessness, irritability, and loss of control and coping mechanisms. There may be an increase in nervousness and general feelings of entrapment. Mental signs include negative attitudes, low self-concept, pessimism, blaming attitudes, and lack of concentration. Left unattended, teachers become increasingly debilitated as they move further into withdrawal.

Teachers enter the education field filled with hope and expectation. If the reflection-and-renewal process is broken, a teacher may begin to withdraw. Without intervention, he or she may slip into deep withdrawal until there is little hope of remaining effective.

Withdrawal can happen at any time during the life of a teacher. It is signaled by a change in the educator's internal motivational drive. He or she begins to withdraw from students, colleagues, and the profession. If they wish to maintain growth, teachers must understand each of these three levels of withdrawal, staying alert for their onset or presence.

Initial Withdrawal

Teachers who enter the danger zone of initial withdrawal may be unaware of what is happening to them. Their teaching continues to be adequate. They remain emotionally committed, although they tend to become more quiet or isolated. Whereas in the past they clearly achieved new levels of competence, the growth that feeds this evolution diminishes. In other words, these teachers stop growing professionally. They become followers rather than leaders. Some even begin to distance themselves physically from the ongoing growth activities of the school. During faculty meetings, these teachers may move to the side or back of the room. When committees are formed to explore new ideas, they wait to be asked instead of being first to volunteer. Initial withdrawal may be related to the internal motivational system of a teacher. Things just do not feel right. The magic is beginning to fade.

Unless these teachers are in tune with themselves, they may not be aware of any changes. An astute administrator, one who knows faculty well, recognizes signs of initial withdrawal and thoughtfully finds ways to invite teachers back into the reflection-and-renewal process. Without intervention, these teachers can slip into the next level of withdrawal.

Persistent Withdrawal

When teachers slip to the level of persistent withdrawal, their negative feelings surface. At this level, teachers become critical of others and unresponsive. Some teachers become overt obstructionists to the ongoing improvement of a school's educational program. They assume a gatekeeper role regarding school reform, literally filtering or deterring important changes they must make in the schoolhouse.

Deep Withdrawal

Teachers who descend into deep withdrawal face a variety of issues. At this level, teachers' professional growth has ceased. They leave the reflection-renewal-growth process behind. As the withdrawal process continues to spiral downward, these teachers tend to become defensive and difficult.

No student should have to endure a teacher in persistent or deep withdrawal. The application of our model to preservice and in-service activities should help prevent teachers from developing the characteristics of persistent and deep withdrawal.

When teachers, students, administrators, and parents work collaboratively, the reflection-and-renewal process can be maintained over the course of a teacher's entire career. By preventing withdrawal, this collaboration can expand the number of expert teachers who guide the educational growth of students. As a guide for professional development, curriculum monitoring, supervision, and teacher-reward systems, the Life Cycle of the Career Teacher model can help administrators identify teachers entering withdrawal.

Other Processes Influencing Teacher Development

The reflection-and-renewal process impacts an educator's professional growth positively, whereas withdrawal impedes that growth. Other factors that influence teacher growth include development issues and social context.

Developmental Issues Influencing the Life Cycle of the Career Teacher Model

The competent, caring, and qualified teacher is foremost a developing person. Issues of development are always at play within the professional context. Three issues are particularly important to consider within the context of the Life Cycle of the Career Teacher model, because they are at work in schools.

Teachers Are Adult Human Beings

Throughout the course of their careers, teachers develop as persons as well as professionals. Developmental, interpersonal, and situational issues in the school may affect performance and the ability to reflect. If a novice teacher, for example, is a young adult, he or she may be grappling with Erikson's (1968) conflicts of intimacy versus isolation while simultaneously trying to work on pedagogical issues. This conflict could lead to problems in relationships with students who may be viewed as a source of teacher support rather than as students to support. Some novice teachers, however, are older, returning students; they face different developmental issues than their young colleagues. Teacher education almost always addresses child development and learning yet rarely addresses adult development and learning. In myriad ways, the notions of adult development and learning impinge on the development of the professional.

Schools Are Developmental Laboratories

Schools are special and unique environments in which persons of multiple ages and various stages of development—teachers and students, young and old, rich and poor, male and female, multiracial, multiethnic, multilinguistic—come together as a community of learners. This extraordinarily rich mixture of learners provides developmental interactions that create both opportunities and conflicts. Whether teachers experience growth or withdrawal may be a function of how development is viewed in the school environment. For example, a professional teacher whose reflections have led to a conflict over his or her inability to influence school changes may not be a good mentor for an eager apprentice unsure of his or her skills. On the other hand, an expert teacher ready to address larger issues of professionalism may be stretched even further by an opportunity to function as a school-university liaison and teacher educator.

Conflict Propels Development

The role of conflict in facilitating development is at the core of most phase and stage theories. An imbalance with one's own point of view—whether from observations, interactions, or experiences—compels the person to reconsider, learn, or grow. In the Life Cycle of the Career Teacher model, reflection and renewal often result in conflict. Changes born from conflicts can be positive and significant for the life of the teacher and the school. Absence of reflection and conflict with one's point of view lead to withdrawal.

Whether the phases of the teaching career advance in a positive direction or get derailed by withdrawal depends on developmental issues. These issues must be considered in each phase of the life cycle. Practices that support general adult development in addition to professional development are necessary for all schools and teachers.

The Influence of Social Contexts on the Life Cycle of the Career Teacher

The contexts in which we live and work and the situations in which we find ourselves also play integral roles in determining who we become and how we function as persons and professionals. Social context is thus a powerful variable influencing teacher development within the Life Cycle of the Career Teacher model. Here, too, three issues are especially significant to consider, because they are at work in schools.

Learning Always Occurs in Changing Social Contexts

Interactions between people and their environments make a difference in whether, what, and how learning occurs, according to research and theory about human learning. In constructivist theories of learning, social context is the environmental variable with the most significant impact on learning. Because this emphasis on learning in social context applies to all people at all points in their development, it reminds us of the important role context plays in determining whether growth or withdrawal will occur. Classroom and school contexts can influence teachers' thinking and behavior. How society views education also can be influential. Because social contexts change over time, learning and growth remain dynamic, fluid, and modifiable over the course of the teaching career. When students demonstrate enthusiasm for a topic, for example, a teacher may be encouraged to learn more about it and develop new classroom activities. However, if that impetus to grow does not occur in the next class, the teacher must identify other ways to maintain learning.

School Cultures Support or Impede Teacher Growth

Interactions with students influence teacher learning, growth, and satisfaction, as do the quality and nature of interactions with colleagues. The successful mentoring of an apprentice or novice teacher by a professional or expert colleague is an important example of how social-context learning assists teacher growth. The climate and culture of a school may support teacher growth in a more pervasive manner than even the most supportive programs for individuals. Having a meaningful voice in decisions about curriculum, professional-development activities, and school goals through a shared decision-making model requires teachers to assume collaborative responsibility and encourages growth throughout the phases of the life-cycle model. Similarly, the absence of shared values, meaningful relationships, and positive interactions among teachers and administrators has a negative impact on teacher learning and development.

Communities and Society Outside School Influence Growth

The extent to which an individual teacher progresses through the phases of the Life Cycle of the Career Teacher model also depends on social contexts beyond the classroom and the school. One such context is a teacher's professional community. Activities connecting teachers to the broader profession through organizations, conferences, and advanced study encourage development across the career via the formation of community. Establishing support groups within a school or partnerships with universities in professional-development schools are other means of development. Another context variable influencing teachers is the policy environment, including local, state, and federal regulations, certification and licensure requirements, and the standards movement. By certifying educators' expertise, the National Board for Professional Teaching Standards (NBPTS, 1994) recognizes teachers improving their practice. Participating in such a community eases the transition from professional to expert teacher. Other influences on teacher growth include societal attitudes, particularly those related to gender and race.

As with developmental issues, the influence of social context must be considered in each phase of the Life Cycle of the Career Teacher model. We must remain mindful of the climate, culture, and community of the school as it supports the professional growth of all the learners within it.

Threads of Continuity: Connections Among the Phases

Consistent with a developmental approach, each progressive phase of the Life Cycle of the Career Teacher model is distinct and unique, building upon those that precede it and providing a foundation for those that follow it. Continuity among the phases, though, is not limited to their sequential relationship to one another. Each phase is bound by two other *threads of continuity* in that each

- Shares the dynamic vision of teaching described throughout this chapter and articulated by the NCTAF (1996) as "competent, caring, and qualified"
- Articulates factors that support and sustain growth in the phase or operate as constraints leading to withdrawal

Competent, Caring, and Qualified Teachers

At each progressive phase of this model, teachers continue to develop as competent, caring, and qualified professionals. It is the definition of those characteristics that evolves and changes with each subsequent phase.

The NCTAF (1996) has viewed this relationship of changing expectations and continuing excellence within the framework of established standards. The commission recommended that prospective teachers be educated in National Council for Accreditation of Teacher Education institutions, inducted into the profession using the framework of the Interstate New Teacher Assessment and Support Consortium, and certified as expert by the NBPTS.

We support the NCTAF's conclusions but also offer other ways of defining changing expectations over time within the concept of the continuity of excellence. Articulating tasks, content, and conflicts that characterize each phase of the Life Cycle of the Career Teacher model strengthens this thread of continuity, a thread that will be elaborated within the chapters addressing each specific phase.

Factors Sustaining Growth or Leading to Withdrawal

We can identify factors that sustain or impede growth at each progressive phase of the Life Cycle of the Career Teacher model. Factors related to the preparation and ongoing professional development of teachers have been summarized in Chapter 1 and will be examined in-depth in subsequent chapters. In this introductory chapter, we have provided a context for discussion of teacher development. We have also discussed connections among the phases and commented on how to use the model.

Chapter 1 provides the structure from which a discussion of each phase can be framed. Chapters 2 through 7 focus on each of the 6 phases of development in the life-cycle model. Each chapter elaborates on a single phase, using a case study to characterize content and tasks, raise issues related to the phase, and focus on the nature of reflection, renewal, and withdrawal within it. Each chapter highlights issues idiosyncratic to the phase and indicates how threads of continuity are reflected.

Recommendations for encouraging phase-related professional growth are offered in each chapter. Each phase-related chapter has the following sections:

- Viewing the Phase Through Case Study
- Defining the Phase
- Threads of Continuity
- Professional-Development Strategies
- Recommendations for Research and Practice

The concluding chapter returns to a holistic look at the Life Cycle of the Career Teacher model. It contains implications and recommendations for the personal and professional growth of teachers across the career, for teacher education across the continuum of practice, for research, for life in schools, and for the ongoing enhancement of the teaching profession.

Uses and Benefits of the Life Cycle of the Career Teacher Model

Our model proposes a developmental theory for teaching across the career. As we mentioned earlier, it must be tested. Teachers may use the model as a gauge for development. They may also view it as a proposal to guide practice. This book offers a career plan to be implemented and evaluated. Hopefully, our model will stimulate thought and action on the shared goal of creating competent, caring, and qualified teachers for all learners.

The NCTAF (1996) envisioned a system in which teachers enter the profession as novices, move through the apprentice and professional phases, and maintain themselves in the expert and distinguished phases. Furthermore, retirees who commit to emeritus activities have clearly internalized the finest qualities we could hope for in our teachers. This Life Cycle of the Career Teacher model can provide the framework to meet and surpass the NCTAF's vision. Benefits of our model include the following:

- Teachers learn that a teaching career involves growth and that they must take steps to ensure movement toward the expert level.
- Administrators support the reflection-renewal-growth process by addressing unique needs of teachers operating in different phases.
- Administrators and teachers become aware of the early signs of withdrawal and work collaboratively to return to the reflection-renewal-growth process.
- Teachers are acknowledged and celebrated for achieving the expert level.
- Teachers entering at the novice and apprentice levels are provided the appropriate support they need to become expert teachers.
- Teachers in withdrawal are encouraged to reflect upon their profession and offered strategies to help them continue to grow.
- The school environment changes into a community in which teachers, administrators, parents, and students are in a continual learning cycle.

In other words, with this model, everyone benefits! Now we must begin the task of applying the model today to improve the classrooms of tomorrow. That journey begins with the elaboration of each of the model's phases.

References

Bell, B., & Gilbert, J. (1996). *Teacher development*. Washington, DC: Falmer.

Boud, D., Keogh, R., & Walker, D. (1985). *Reflections: Turning experience into learning*. London: Logan Page.

Dewey, J. (1910). *How we think*. New York: D. C. Heath.
Erikson, E. H. (1968). *Identity, youth, and crisis.* New York: W. W. Norton.
Fuller, F. F. (1969). Concerns of teachers: A developmental conceptualization. *American Educational Research Journal, 6*(2), 208–226.
Gehrke, N. J. (1987). *On being a teacher*. West Lafayette, IN: Kappa Delta Pi, an International Honor Society in Education.
Grimmett, P. P., & Erickson, G. L. (1988). *Reflection in teacher education*. New York: Teachers College Press.
Haberman, M. (1995). *Star teachers of children in poverty*. West Lafayette, IN: Kappa Delta Pi, an International Honor Society in Education.
Huberman, A. M., Grounauer, M., & Marti, J. (1993). *The lives of teachers* (J. Neufeld, Trans.). New York: Teachers College Press.
Katz, L. G. (1977). *Talks with teachers: Reflections on early childhood education*. Washington, DC: National Association for the Education of Young Children.
Levine, S. L. (1989). *Promoting adult growth in schools: The promise of professional development*. Boston: Allyn & Bacon.
Levinson, D. J., Darrow, C. N., Klein, E. B., Levinson, M. H., & McKee, B. (1978). *The seasons of a man's life.* New York: Knopf.
Loevinger, J. (1987). *Paradigms of personality*. New York: Freeman.
Lortie, D. C. (1975). *Schoolteacher: A sociological study*. Chicago: University of Chicago Press.
Loughran, J. (1996). *Developing reflective practice: Learning about teaching and learning through modeling*. Washington, DC: Falmer.
National Board for Professional Teaching Standards. (1994). *What teachers should know and be able to do*. Detroit: Author.
National Commission on Teaching and America's Future. (1996). What matters most: Teaching for America's future. New York: Author. ERIC ED 395 931
Osterman, K. F., & Kottkamp, R. B. (1993). *Reflective practice for educators: Improving schooling through professional development*. Newbury Park, CA: Corwin.
Piaget, J. (1954). *The construction of reality in the child* (M. Cook, Trans.). New York: Basic Books.
Pines, A. M., Aronson, E., & Kafrey, D. (1981). *Burnout: From tedium to personal growth.* New York: Free Press.
Schön, D. A. (1983). *The reflective practitioner: How professionals think in action*. New York: Basic Books.
Schön, D. A. (1987). *Educating the reflective practitioner*. San Francisco: Jossey-Bass.
Steffy, B. E. (1989). *Career stages of classroom teachers.* Lancaster, PA: Technomic.
Steffy, B. E., & Wolfe, M. P. (1997). *The life cycle of the career teacher: Main-*

taining excellence for a lifetime. West Lafayette, IN: Kappa Delta Pi, an International Honor Society in Education.

Valli, L., (Ed.) (1997). *Reflective teacher education: Cases and critiques.* Albany: State University of New York Press.

VanderVen, K. (1988). Pathways to professional effectiveness for early childhood educators. In B. Spodek, O. N. Saracho, and D. L. Peters (Eds.), *Professionalism and the early childhood practitioner* (pp. 137–160). New York: Teachers College Press.

Yager, R. E. (1991). The constructivist learning model. *Science Teacher, 58*(6), 52–57.

Zeichner, K. M. (1994). Educational reform and teacher knowledge. In S. Hollingsworth and H. Sockett (Eds.), *Teacher research and educational reform: 97th yearbook of the National Society for the Study of Education* (pp. 66–84). Chicago: University of Chicago Press.

Zeichner, K. M., Tabachnik, B. R., & Densmore, K. (1987). Individual, institutional, and cultural influences on the development of teachers' craft knowledge. In J. Calderhead (Ed.), *Exploring teachers' thinking* (pp. 21–59). London: Cassell.

2 The Novice Teacher

by Michael J. Berson and Rick A. Breault

Viewing the Novice Phase Through Case Study

As an undergraduate majoring in social studies education, Anthony had just completed 3½ years of coursework. Espousing child-centered, multicultural views that supported a constructivist model of learning, he appeared to be a stellar preservice education student. In his methods classes, he was praised for his creativity and zeal for social studies. Full of energy and idealism, Anthony began his student teaching internship at a middle school in an economically impoverished neighborhood. He was excited about his placement, because it offered him an environment in which his skills would be challenged and his résumé enhanced. Success in this setting could ease the path to a job offer for the subsequent school year. Anthony was to instruct seventh-grade classes in geography, a social studies area he enjoyed. Still, with only one geography course completed during his undergraduate training, he was concerned that he needed to work on content.

The university Anthony attended featured a weekly educational seminar that accompanied internships. At the first meeting, Anthony was introduced to his supervisor, a retired middle school principal with more than 33 years of experience. In addition to providing support to interns during the seminars, she would conduct six field visits and assign a grade at the end of the internship. During their initial meeting, the supervisor emphasized that his internship was an opportunity to experiment, take risks, and be creative. When she learned he was proficient at integrating technology into his social studies instruction, she encouraged Anthony to continue developing technology as a tool in his seventh-grade classroom. In fact, she admired efforts to try innovative methods and learn from both successes and failures.

Anthony's next step was to meet officially with his cooperating teacher, Mr. Jamison, whom he had met previously during a practicum observation. They arranged two meetings prior to the start of the internship to become more acquainted and to give the student teacher additional opportunities to observe Mr. Jamison and his students in action. From the beginning, Anthony liked the way the teacher maintained order in the classroom and kept students on-task. He was awed by Mr. Jamison's ease in moving between lessons and discipline.

Preparing for his transition to classroom teacher, Anthony was determined to wow his students with exciting lessons and to amaze his cooperating teacher with superior teaching skills. He perceived that many of Mr. Jamison's instructional strategies lacked uniqueness and tended to be driven by the course textbook. Anthony spent a lot of time planning for instruction, staying up late prepping for his classes. In his journal, he noted that fatigue had become a constant sensation in his everyday life. His exhaustion soon translated into impatience and intolerance.

Anthony's initial attempts to instruct classes met with mixed results. Within the first week, his authority was challenged by a student who matched his height and size. When he looked around the classroom for support, Anthony realized Mr. Jamison had not yet returned from the principal's office. In subsequent weeks, the intern frequently was interrupted by discipline problems, rarely making it through an entire lesson plan. He almost always went home with the feeling of not having accomplished much. To preserve valuable class time, Anthony began addressing class disturbances superficially. He soon found himself relying on more traditional forms of instruction.

Although initially excited to integrate technology throughout his instruction and already successful in developing exceptional lesson plans, Anthony discovered that his classroom was equipped with just one computer not connected to the Internet. Moreover, he would be unable to access the hardware available during his coursework at the university.

Some of Anthony's lessons were successful, such as his collaborative-group project to construct a map identifying centers of food production throughout the world. However, other lessons prepared with the same care and considerations fell apart. After discussing his successes and failures with his university supervisor and cooperating teacher, there was consensus between the supervisor and Anthony that he had indeed accomplished a great deal and engaged students most successfully when he used hands-on activities in the geography classroom. Mr. Jamison, however, believed hands-on projects were too time-consuming and yielded too few results in the area of learning.

Anthony decided to go with his teaching preferences and implement more hands-on activities in geography. During the remainder of his internship, he found that students enjoyed these activities, but he often faced criticism by the cooperating teacher and the principal for "an out-of-control classroom." Anthony conceded that, in his attempt to try out different ways of teaching, he had abandoned structure and consistency.

The biggest blow to Anthony's internship experience came after he administered and scored his first unit test. The students had performed miserably. Anthony met with his university supervisor and cooperating teacher, who concluded that he relied too much on the test package accompanying the textbook to generate his assessment instrument. This strategy did not reflect the instructional tasks and knowledge base the students had been developing throughout Anthony's involvement in their classes. Mr. Jamison expressed concern that the students were not learning enough of the content.

Seven weeks into his internship, Anthony had become quite disillusioned. He was overwhelmed with concurrently juggling the needs of 115 seventh-grade students, preparing lesson plans, grading assignments, developing his résumé, and being evaluated. Reviewing his journal entries, he saw himself engaging in the very behaviors he condemned as marks of poor teaching—relying more on the textbook to guide his lesson development and disciplining students with threats and a raised voice. Anthony initially believed his young age would allow students to connect with him as a peer; heading into week eight, he viewed himself as another bossy grown-up who ordered his students to complete irrelevant activities.

The intern spent long hours at the library and on the Internet looking up background information and reading the text to stay ahead of his students. Attempting to cover as much content as possible, Anthony began talking at his students during the 50-minute class periods. Glassy stares, drooping eyes, and even snores told him that he was boring rather than insightful. Still, he felt energized during those fleeting moments when he believed a connection had been made with a student, such as when he found a note one day on top of his geography book. The note read, "Thank you Mr. K. for the help on my project. You are my favorite teacher. I like your ties. Can you teach me to tie mine for the music recital on Wednesday? —Andres."

Defining the Novice Phase

Anthony is representative of a novice teacher by function of his developmental stage and experience. He has successfully completed his practica and continues to evolve his skills in the full-time student teaching internship. Like many novice teachers, Anthony experiences a range of emotions regarding his induction into the teaching profession. His idealism is accompanied by anxiety, frustration, disillusionment, elation, fear, and insecurity. He still is in need of mentorship, especially because he remains naive regarding many of the organizational, administrative, and interpersonal forces that impact teachers. The internship is Anthony's first intensive exposure to, as Rust (1994) described it,

> the delicate balance of competing demands that beset teachers daily, even hourly; the hours of planning and thinking about teaching that are required to make interactive learning possible; the networking that is necessary to develop a support system in the school and in the profession; the subtleties of classroom design and classroom management that make it possible for children to assume responsibility for their actions; and the political sensibilities that are essential for survival and for change in the schools. (p. 216)

The novice phase comprises that period of time when the individual has begun orientation to the teaching profession. This orientation involves a process initiated with experiences in practica and evolving throughout the student teaching internship. The essential developmental task of this phase is exploration and expansion of one's perspectives. Preservice teachers acquire a knowledge base that incorporates subject content, pedagogy, and professionalism. This process requires enormous reserves of courage, energy, tolerance for ambiguity, and a willingness to take risk. The novice teacher engages in the exploration of available possibilities, formulates a fledgling definition of self as a teacher, and initiates the complicated transition from receiving ongoing supervision of day-to-day activities to independent functioning as a professional. This need to acquire independence may contribute to ambivalent feelings about turning to supervisors for advice and support during periods of high stress.

Novice teachers may be confused and even overwhelmed by the clash of their expectations for teaching and the reality of life in the classroom and school. They quite suddenly are immersed in a context of contrasts. They are placed in a role preoccupied with outward appearance as classroom performers. They often are so consumed with looking like teachers that they miss understanding the complexities of student behavior. Novices typically enter their internships with unexamined assumptions about pedagogy. Their overreliance on a rigid belief system can prevent them from recognizing that their decisions and actions will be publicly scrutinized (Howey & Zimpher, 1996).

As a novice teacher, Anthony is consumed by the task of organizing the instructional content. Although he desires excellence, he struggles to achieve competence in the classroom. He focuses on designing the perfect activity or assignment but lacks a broader sense of what it means to learn, to be educated, and to engage in the process of intellectual and personal growth (Metzger, 1996). As a preservice education student, Anthony had been energized by professors who made him responsible for his own thinking. However, Anthony confused his own empowerment to learn as a substitute for experience.

Alternative Models of Preparation

Though Anthony represents a typical preservice teacher, trends toward alternative teacher certification and the recruitment of teachers from other professions make characterizing the needs of the novice more difficult than other phases. The combination of traditional and nontraditional routes into teaching means that a preservice teacher might be anyone from a 45-year-old career naval officer who had thousands of young people under his command to an 18-year-old woman who has never left her small Midwestern town but wants to teach because she enjoys baby-sitting her siblings. Both might be at the novice phase, but the strategies for supporting growth and preventing withdrawal may be vastly different for each.

The situation is also complicated by a wide range of teacher-preparation options. The ex-naval officer might take several years of a traditional teacher education curriculum with extensive field experiences. The 18-year-old might graduate with a degree in mathematics, take a couple of summer courses in educational psychology and pedagogy, serve a semester-long internship with a mentor of questionable quality, and then be sent to a population of disadvantaged urban students to practice her new skills. It is nearly impossible to predict which of these candidates will survive and grow and which will not last the year.

Transitions From School to Work Environments

The two experiences that most novices share is exposure to some kind of preparatory coursework through a school of education and supervised field experiences in an elementary, middle, or secondary school. In these settings, either the basis for and tendency toward professional growth is established or the inadequacy of preparation and poor advising sows the seeds of early withdrawal. When considering how to nurture growth or prevent withdrawal, it is important to study controllable factors, particularly the teacher education curriculum and the nature of early field experiences. It will help to review some dominant characteristics and assumptions in current teacher education programs that either help or hinder the transition to apprenticeship.

Teacher educators, at least as far back as Dewey (1904, 1910, 1938), have voiced the importance of preparing teachers with a repertoire of skills they can apply to address the needs of a variety of students. More recently, Apple (1996), Bernstein (1990), and Liston and Zeichner (1991) addressed the need for teachers to view their work as culturally situated and to feel empowered as change agents and decision makers. The curriculum and methods used by some teacher educators, however, not only fail to meet these criteria but, in many cases, discourage the development of important characteristics. Understanding why this failure occurs is important, because traits such as reflectivity and independent decision making are key to professional growth and success.

In the case study, Anthony experienced something for which teacher education programs too often do not prepare their graduates—the reality of school life. Veenman (1984, p. 143) called it a reality check, a point at which a novice teacher suffers "the collapse of the missionary ideals formed during teacher training by the harsh and rude reality of everyday classroom life." If the events producing the reality check are serious enough and not addressed in any meaningful way, the result can be early withdrawal from teaching. At the very least, the novice's attempt to reduce the dissonance created by bureaucratic norms, structural characteristics of schooling, and teacher reference groups can lead to a retrenchment into more conservative or custodial views of teaching (Buchmann, 1990; Bullough, 1992; Veenman, 1984; Wideen, Mayersmith, & Moon, 1998). What Anthony experienced was not a rare occurrence. Even if a preservice teacher takes on numerous early field experiences, the length and immersion of the student teaching or internship almost always exposes a tension between classroom reality and the relevance of the teacher education program.

Despite many reforms in recent years, teacher education still relies heavily on what might be called "propositional knowledge"—campus-based coursework and information about teaching methods delivered in a relatively passive manner. Strong arguments can be made about the importance of providing a solid background in subject matter as well as the foundational and theoretical aspects of teaching (Bullough, 1992; Feiman-Nemser & Buchmann, 1989; Goodlad, 1990). However, the way in which information is communicated to future teachers many times prevents its integration into classroom teaching. As Buchmann and Schwille (1983, p. 31) observed, "First-hand experience is trusted implicitly as both the means and content of education. It is 'down to earth,' personal, sensory, and practical. Ideas encountered in books are pale in contrast." Too often, teacher educators advocate the practice of constructivist teaching but do not use it. They fail to recognize the powerful beliefs and assumptions with which preservice teachers enter their professional preparation. In the process, teacher educators frequently miss opportunities to connect theory to practice or unintentionally reinforce the limiting perspectives held by the novices.

Three areas of the novice experience typically are addressed inadequately during preservice preparation: the complexity of school culture, the nurturing of reflective practice, and the taken-for-granted assumptions of preservice teachers. When student teachers enter the classroom, they find the environment anything but isolated. At every step, classroom decisions are influenced by administrative guidelines, funding limitations, community pressure, parental concern, state politics, and more. The novice brings to the situation idealism, enthusiasm, and good ideas but very few "street smarts." Many teacher educators, however, insist on putting the burden of reform on the backs of new teachers, setting them up as martyrs in a crusade to implement dozens of innovative practices (Breault, in press). As Wideen et al. (1998) described the situation,

> The practical pressure of the student teaching experience appears to limit the ability and inclination of preservice teachers to do anything other than just survive. . . . Meanwhile, the change agenda of the teacher educators remain and exacerbate the differences between the perceptions of the faculty member and those of the teaching candidates. (p. 156)

For most beginning teachers, the best they can do is to muddle through their first year and gain the experience needed to make sense of their work in the classroom. Novices enter an occupation in which action is imperative. They have good reasons for insisting that what they most need to do is "to learn to act and talk as classroom teachers" (Bird, Anderson, Sullivan, & Swidler 1993, p. 266).

It is no surprise that the novice regularly falls back on existing curricula, textbook suggestions, and an emphasis on classroom control. Yet many teacher educators provide methods courses that encourage remaking the curriculum in every subject area and meeting the needs of every child instead of encouraging incremental changes in the context of the school culture and the first year of teaching. Weinstein (1988) has gone so far as to claim that teacher educators are guilty of "dumbing down" the act of teaching by overemphasizing the notion that learning is nonproblematic if certain methods are applied. Young teachers many times are encouraged to find their own personal teaching style that "feels right" to them; too often, discussion of what to do when faced with failure is avoided. As Weinstein (1988, p. 31) noted, "The implication is that teaching is instinctive rather than learned, that there are no particular patterns of behavior that are more effective than others." Research suggests that preservice teachers prepared within a professional-development site are more adept at succeeding on their own; yet even in these cases the quality of the experience is crucial (Levine, 1992; Lewis & Walling, 1996; Powell & McGowan, 1995).

Teacher educators are not solely to blame for the tension experienced by novice teachers; an equal share of responsibility rests with schools in which student teachers learn their craft. Rather than focusing more intensely on professional issues, risk taking, and critical reflection, field experiences too often teach beginners to be docile and reflect the values of those in charge (Ginsburg & Clift, 1990). Characteristics valued in the school site many times are in opposition to those valued by the university and, to some extent, the beginning teacher (Darling-Hammond, 1994; Veenman, 1984). Many early field experiences also suffer from inflexible or poorly trained cooperating teachers, difficult logistics, poor communication, and a school culture that reinforces or legitimates existing practices and assumptions (Feiman-Nemser & Buchmann, 1989; Giebelhaus & Bowman, 1996; Ginsburg & Clift, 1990; Hult & Edens, 1998).

The beginning teacher tends to have progressive, humanistic ideas about educating children, but those beliefs largely emerge during the university years and rarely become as deeply rooted as other, more conservative, notions of teaching. Most preservice teachers value the learning that occurs through firsthand experience more than the structured discourse of the university (Bolin, 1990; Buchmann & Schwille, 1983; Howey & Zimpher, 1996). New teachers soon learn that schools want stable, competent, and responsible teachers. At this stage in their career, new teachers simply want to fit in with other teachers (Alexander, Muir, & Chant, 1992). Given these considerations, when field experiences call into question any innovative methods or understanding of child development as suggested in coursework, the novice must choose between pleasing a university supervisor with the power to grade or a future employer reflecting the power of the marketplace. There is no easy choice.

Threads of Continuity

The pressure to conform during field experiences has led to an inadequate development of critical-reflection skills. An ability to consider and articulate one's instructional decisions is not just an altruistic goal for the experienced teacher; it is crucial for preservice teachers who will seek licenses in states adopting standards, such as those Darling-Hammond (1992) suggested in an Interstate New Teacher Assessment and Support Consortium (INTASC) paper. Critical consideration and application of student knowledge, assessment practice, cultural diversity, school personnel, and the community—skills recommended in INTASC standards—are not intuitive or instinctual; they are learned abilities that must be observed and practiced. Preservice teachers need experience as early as possible in settings that model inquiry, collegiality, trust, risk taking, and support, yet they seldom find it in traditional field experiences (Bliss & Mazur, 1997; Conle, 1996; Giebelhaus & Bowman, 1996; Levine, 1992; Powell & McGowan, 1995).

Despite their general academic atmosphere, many universities fail to nurture critical thinking among future teachers. Campus rhetoric is filled with references about the need for reflection, but the importance given to theory once coursework overlaps with field experiences and methodology is limited. The problem rests not so much with the lack of theoretical content as it does with the lack of deliberate linking of theory to practice as well as not providing experiences and activities in which that can happen. Students rarely receive adequate time for reflection or have critically reflective teaching modeled for them by classroom teachers or college professors (Ginsburg & Clift, 1990; Howey & Zimpher, 1996). Bolin (1990) found that reflective tools such as journals are not treated seriously by university supervisors, instead becoming tedious exercises to insulate oneself from facing tough questions. Teacher educators seem to operate on the assumption that, once provided with a theoretical background and field experiences, preservice teachers will make theory-practice connections on their own. Most will not (Carter, 1990; Feiman-Nemser & Buchmann, 1989).

The Role of Prior Beliefs

One of the most powerful factors determining the success or failure of a novice teacher's transition to the apprentice phase is the set of beliefs that person brings with them and how those beliefs become altered by the teacher education experience. Again, traditional approaches to teacher education have placed emphasis on propositional knowledge, leading to the trivializing or even neglect of students' deeply held beliefs (Howey & Zimpher, 1996). Failure to integrate consideration of these beliefs and past experiences into theoretical coursework and current field experiences likely reinforces the perception that teacher education programs are generally irrelevant (Alexander et al., 1992; Bolin, 1990; Lortie, 1975).

Teacher education is sometimes viewed as a delaying tactic on what novices see as a "subjective warrant to teach" (Lortie, 1975, p. 39). This view especially is prevalent among elementary education majors, who typically cite "warmth," "patience," and "a love of children" as personal qualities that will make them good teachers. They assume that common sense, their own school memories, and a teacher's guide will supply the subject matter necessary to educate students and that teacher education courses will help them acquire a few instructional techniques and classroom control methods (Wideen et al., 1998). From that perspective, the teacher educator is viewed as someone who joins an existing conversation, changes the topic, and expects enthusiastic participation. Many teacher educators assume preservice teachers will take the principles of the profession as a given against which to adjust their student-based beliefs and points of view. In reality, few preservice teachers think about their future instruction by using research-based rationales to predict possible effects of instructional decisions. Many assume that the principles of the profession are ideas to prove against the givens of their student-based beliefs (Holt-Reynolds, 1991). Even if their ideas are inadequate, the rationales cannot be discounted because of the central role they play in decision making and how they define effective teaching.

Novice teachers use their prior beliefs as a kind of interpretative lens through which they process or "read" new information about teaching and decide what is practical and possible (Alexander et al., 1992; Bird et al., 1993; Bramald, Hardman, & Leat, 1995; Holt-Reynolds, 1991). Though those beliefs are deeply rooted, tacitly held, and not easily changed, evidence supports the possibility of altering or increasing the sophistication of the belief structure through preservice education (Bramald et al., 1995; Bullough, 1992; Levin & Ammon, 1992; Wideen et al., 1998). By identifying and examining prior beliefs early in the preparation process and introducing new conceptions of teaching and learning in relation to existing personal schema, new teachers might be more able and likely to assimilate theoretical considerations and research findings into their instructional decision making.

The benefits of easing the novice-to-apprentice transition are threefold: First, the new openness to theory and research could lessen tensions between the school and the university, thereby lessening feelings of inadequacy or incompetence. Second, the increased self-knowledge and ability to integrate theory and practice could improve critical reflection as well as provide a larger repertoire of strategies with which to solve classroom problems. Third, as teacher educators gain insight into the pedagogical conceptions and significant past events of preservice teachers, they will better identify what Levin and Ammon (1992) called "leverage points" to help future teachers grow and develop in needed areas.

Making Good Use of Prior Experiences

Researchers have suggested a number of ways in which teacher educators can help bring prior beliefs to the surface and therefore integrate them into teacher preparation. Preservice teachers must make explicit the beliefs they hold and come to see these beliefs as rooted in their own experiences, homes, communities, and schooling. Among the more successful means of accomplishing this goal are biographical or metaphorical activities (Bullough, 1992; Conle, 1996; Veenman, 1984). Holt-Reynolds (1991) suggested the following activities for teacher educators to use in helping preservice teachers mine their beliefs:

- Conduct discussions in which students are asked to support their points of view by making explicit connections to life-history events and the interpretation of those events.
- Incorporate analytical discourse assignments, such as Myself-as-Experienced-Student and Myself-as-Inexperienced-Teacher.
- Develop greater knowledge of others as learners through tutoring and case studies.
- Describe the decision-making and reflective processes used in developing course syllabi, readings, and activities.

Professional-Development Strategies

Painting such a discouraging picture of the status of teacher education may leave readers feeling like Dickens's (1923, p. 144) Ebenezer Scrooge asking the Ghost of Christmas Yet to Come, "Are these the shadows of things that Will be, or are they shadows of the things that May be only?" Several trends in the preparation of teachers offer some promise, as Scrooge hoped, that, "if [present] courses be departed from, the ends will change." A change in course alone, however, is not sufficient if those changes are inadequately examined and do not address the problems already mentioned.

Active school-university partnerships such as the Professional Development School (PDS) movement have gained momentum in the past decade and a half. Today's variations on the PDS model can be found in many, if not most, teacher education programs. The potential of these partnerships to offer a more effective transition into the teaching profession is great, but the creation of optimal conditions in such a partnership is a complex process (Berry, Boles, Edens, Nissenholtz, & Trachtman, 1996; Hult & Edens, 1998; Teitel, 1996).

Professional-development sites, with their strong emphasis on the relationship between teacher, student, and preservice as well as inservice learning, can provide a unique environment in which the pedagogy of professional development is congruent with the pedagogy desired in the classroom (Acquarelli & Mumme, 1996; Hult & Edens, 1998). School-based experiences provided through partnerships can immerse preservice teachers in the full context of the school and induct them into the profession more effectively than traditional campus-based programs (Lewis & Walling, 1996; Lieberman & Miller, 1990). Most important, an active school-university partnership can demonstrate the integration of theory into practice and the contribution of practice to theory.

These changes, however, do not guarantee the implementation of new ideas by novices once they begin teaching (Levin & Ammon, 1992; Wideen et al., 1998). Novices must be able both to make their thinking explicit and demonstrate their thinking in practice. Portfolio development could fulfill both of those roles, but increased research is needed on the content of the portfolios and the processes by which they are developed. A teacher education program that prepares novice teachers to move more smoothly and successfully through each career cycle is one that prepares them for transition. Each cycle brings with it a change in professional thinking, but the most drastic transition is probably that which the novice experiences—the transition from student to professional. Portfolios, if used effectively, can build the level of self-knowledge and sense of responsibility needed during that transition (Antonek, McCormick, & Donato, 1997; Sherbet, 1996–1997).

Recommendations for Research and Practice

Field experiences, whether in a partnership school or any other setting, are probably the most meaningful component of formal teacher education. Knowles, Cole, and Presswood (1994, p. 96), invoking the spirit of Dewey, have qualified that assertion by adding that "it is not enough to just have an experience or engage in activities; everything depends on the quality of the experience that is had, not only how agreeable it is but also how it influences later experiences." The second area of recommended research, then, is to explore variations on the traditional one-class/one-teacher placement and learning "by the seat of your pants" emphasis in field experiences. Given the amount of time university faculty members now spend in the field, more effort must be put into finding out what happens during that time and what results emerge from field experiences.

Goodlad (1990, p. 281) offered one of the earliest and strongest criticisms of this model, calling the placement of a neophyte in a single classroom with a single cooperating teacher "a seriously flawed approach" that "does not prepare future teachers to be stewards of entire schools." His preference was for students to be assigned to schools rather than classrooms, much like a medical student is assigned to a hospital rather than a specific person.

Carter (1990) argued that natural classroom settings can be quite confusing, suggesting that novices might well direct their attention to irrelevant aspects of the stream of action. As Carter (1990) noted:

> Constructed and guided experiences designed on the basis of an analytical understanding of teaching events are often more instructive than natural settings because the essential cognitive dimensions are more easily accessible. Such experiences, in turn, provide the cognitive foundation for knowledge construction in more natural environments. (p. 307)

Similarly, Bolin (1990, p. 17) recommended that student teaching should become more of a "protected experience in which the student can pause from the regular demands of life and focus intensely on professional issues." In that way, the experience can nurture self-reflection and a deepening perspective about oneself.

Challenging the traditional view of field experience, a number of studies have found that the traditional student teaching triad of preservice teacher, cooperating teacher, and university supervisor often fosters an unreflective and uncritical training experience. Even when student teachers demonstrate an obvious lack of subject-matter knowledge, neither cooperating teachers nor university supervisors notice or choose to comment on it (Feiman-Nemser & Buchmann, 1989). Similarly, Zeichner and Liston (1985), Geibelhaus and Bowman (1996), Grimmett and Ratzlaff (1986), and Mackin and Klindienst (1998) suggested that cooperating teachers are many times unprepared as supervisors and therefore tentative in their feedback. Furthermore, many university supervisors are unprepared to offer meaningful feedback.

The Life Cycle of the Career Teacher model has important implications for teacher educators and mentors who work with novices. It requires seeing preservice education as one end of a continuum that spans the entire career of a teacher; indeed, the first step in an evolutionary process. Early preservice coursework and field experiences should be designed with the successful completion of student teaching in mind. Student teaching, the transition time between the novice and apprentice phases, should improve the odds that the apprentice will make it past the first few years of teaching, enter the professional phase, and move through all phases of the cycle.

The characteristics nurtured in future teachers must go beyond teaching techniques to frames of mind or dispositions that will serve them well throughout their career. Teacher educators must reexamine the ways their programs communicate realistic expectations for new teachers in complex environments, provide field experiences that honor both theory and practice, and develop critically reflective practitioners. Only by paying close attention to these factors will teacher educators help novices convert their idealism, conservative backgrounds, self-confidence, and uncertainty into survival skills that can withstand disillusionment and burnout, both of which can prematurely end or limit professional life.

References

Acquarelli, K., & Mumme, J. (1996). A renaissance in mathematics education reform. *Phi Delta Kappan, 77*(7), 478–482, 484.

Alexander, D., Muir, D., & Chant, D. (1992). Interrogating stories: How teachers think they learned to teach. *Teaching & Teacher Education,*

8(1), 59–68.

Antonek, J. L., McCormick, D. E., & Donato, R. (1997). The student teacher portfolio as autobiography: Developing a professional identity. *Modern Language Journal, 81*(1), 15–27.

Apple, M. W. (1996). *Cultural politics and education.* New York: Teachers College Press.

Bernstein, B. (1990). *The structuring of pedagogic discourse, Vol. 4: Class, codes, and control.* London: Routledge.

Berry, B., Boles, K., Edens, K., Nissenholtz, A., & Trachtman, R. (1996). *Inquiry and professional development schools.* Paper presented for the National Center for Restructuring Education, Schools, and Teaching, Teachers College, Columbia University, New York.

Bird, T., Anderson, L. M., Sullivan, B. A., & Swidler, S. A. (1993). Pedagogical balancing acts: Attempts to influence prospective teachers' beliefs. *Teaching & Teacher Education, 9*(3), 253–267.

Bliss, T., & Mazur, J. (1997, February). *How INTASC standards come alive through case studies.* Paper presented at the annual conference of the American Association of Colleges of Teacher Education, Phoenix, AZ.

Bolin, F. S. (1990). Helping student teachers think about teaching: Another look at Lou. *Journal of Teacher Education, 41*(1), 10–19.

Bramald, R., Hardman, F., & Leat, D. (1995). Initial teacher trainees and their views of teaching and learning. *Teaching & Teacher Education, 11*(1), 23–31.

Breault, R. A. (in press). The sound bite curriculum. *The Teacher Educator.*

Buchmann, M. (1990). *Making new or making do: An inconclusive argument about teaching* (Issue paper 90-7). East Lansing, MI: National Center for Research on Teacher Learning. ERIC ED 325 457

Buchmann, M., & Schwille, J. R. (1983). Education: The overcoming of experience. *American Journal of Education, 92*(1), 30–51.

Bullough, R. V., Jr. (1992). Beginning teacher curriculum decision making, personal teaching metaphors, and teacher education. *Teaching & Teacher Education, 8*(3), 239–252.

Carter, K. (1990). Teachers' knowledge and learning to teach. In W. R. Houston (Ed.), *Handbook of research on teacher education* (pp. 291–310). New York: Macmillan.

Conle, C. (1996). Resonance in preservice teacher inquiry. *American Educational Research Journal, 33*(2), 297–325.

Darling-Hammond, L. (Ed.). (1992). *Model standards for beginning teacher licensing and development: A resource for state dialogue.* Unpublished paper. Washington, DC: Interstate New Teacher Assessment and

Support Consortium.

Darling-Hammond, L. (1994). *Professional development schools: Schools for developing a profession.* New York: Teachers College Press.

Dewey, J. (1904). The relation of theory to practice. In C. Murray (Ed.), *The third NSSE yearbook: Part I* (pp. 15–25). Chicago: University of Chicago Press.

Dewey, J. (1910). *How we think.* Buffalo, NY: Prometheus.

Dewey, J. (1938). *Experience and education.* New York: Macmillan.

Dickens, C. (1923). *A Christmas carol.* New York: Macmillan.

Feiman-Nemser, S., & Buchmann, M. (1989). Describing teacher education: A framework and illustrative findings from a longitudinal study of six students. *Elementary School Journal, 89*(3), 365–378.

Giebelhaus, C. R., & Bowman, C. (1996, October). *The impact of cooperating teacher training on the professional development of student teachers.* Paper presented at the annual conference of the Mid-Western Educational Research Association, Chicago.

Ginsburg, M. B., & Clift, R. T. (1990). The hidden curriculum of preservice teacher education. In W. R. Houston (Ed.), *Handbook of research on teacher education* (pp. 450–650). New York: Macmillan.

Goodlad, J. I. (1990). *Teachers for our nation's schools.* San Francisco: Jossey-Bass.

Grimmett, P. P., & Ratzlaff, H. C. (1986). Expectations for the cooperating teacher role. *Journal of Teacher Education, 37*(6), 41–50.

Holt-Reynolds, D. (1991). *The dialogues of teacher education: Entering and influencing preservice teachers' internal conversations.* (Research Report 91-4). East Lansing, MI: National Center for Research on Teacher Learning. ERIC ED 337 459

Howey, K. R., & Zimpher, N. (1996). Patterns in prospective teachers: Guides for designing preservice programs. In F. B. Murray (Ed.), *The teacher educator's handbook* (pp. 465–505). San Francisco: Jossey-Bass.

Hult, R. E., & Edens, K. M. (1998, April). *Collaboration: A key to success of early field experiences.* Paper presented at the annual meeting of the American Educational Research Association, San Diego.

Knowles, J. G., Cole, A. L., & Presswood, C. S. (1994). *Through preservice teachers' eyes: Exploring field experiences through narrative and inquiry.* New York: Merrill.

Levin, B. B., & Ammon, P. (1992). The development of beginning teachers' pedagogical thinking: A longitudinal analysis of four case studies. *Teacher Education Quarterly, 19*(4), 19–37.

Levine, M. (Ed.). (1992). *Professional practice schools: Linking teacher education and school reform.* New York: Teachers College Press.

Lewis, M., & Walling, B. (1996, April). *Development of professional identity among professional development school preservice teachers: Longitudinal and comparative analysis.* Paper presented at the annual meeting of the American Educational Research Association, New York.

Lieberman, A., & Miller, L. (1990). Teacher development in professional practice schools. *Teachers College Record, 92*(1), 105–122.

Liston, D. P., & Zeichner, K. M. (1991). *Teacher education and the social conditions of schooling*. New York: Routledge.

Lortie, D. C. (1975). *Schoolteacher: A sociological study*. Chicago: The University of Chicago Press.

Mackin, J., & Klindienst, D. B. (1998, April). *Creating a community of science educators: Perceptions of preservice teachers and inservice teachers on their professional development experiences.* Paper presented at the annual conference of the American Educational Research Association, San Diego, CA.

Metzger, M. (1996). Maintaining a life. *Phi Delta Kappan, 77*(5), 346–351.

Powell, J. H., & McGowan, T. M. (1995). Adjusting the focus: Teachers' roles and responsibilities in a school/university collaborative. *Teacher Educator, 31*(1), 1–22.

Rust, F. O. (1994). The first year of teaching: It's not what they expected. *Teaching & Teacher Education, 10*(2), 205–217.

Sherbet, S. (1996–1997). Portfolio development: A journey from student to professional. *Career Planning & Adult Development Journal, 12*(4), 35–39.

Teitel, L. (1996). *NCATE PDS standards literature review.* Washington, DC: National Council for Accreditation of Teacher Education.

Veenman, S. (1984). Perceived problems of beginning teachers. *Review of Educational Research, 54*(2), 143–178.

Weinstein, C. S. (1988). Preservice teachers' expectations about the first year of teaching. *Teaching & Teacher Education, 4*(1), 31–41.

Wideen, M., Mayersmith, J., & Moon, B. (1998). A critical analysis of the research on learning to teach: Making the case for an ecological perspective on inquiry. *Review of Educational Research, 68*(2), 130–178.

Zeichner, K., & Liston, D. (1985). Varieties of discourse in supervisory conference. *Teaching & Teacher Education, 1*(2), 155–174.

3 The Apprentice Teacher

by Mary C. Clement, Billie J. Enz, and George E. Pawlas

Viewing the Apprentice Phase Through Case Study

Tom's Case

Tom landed his first teaching assignment midway through the fall semester. Eager to become a full-time, full-fledged teacher, he excitedly toured the school where his knowledge and skills would be put into practice. As the apprentice and the principal approached the classroom assigned to Tom, they witnessed students throwing items at one another, including newly purchased textbooks. Instead of becoming involved and helping the substitute teacher, the principal simply closed the door and refocused the conversation on other topics.

After accepting the principal's offer to join the faculty as a ninth-grade science teacher at a large middle school, Tom learned he was the fourth science teacher to take the position in the past 5 years. The teaching schedule required him, like his predecessors, to prepare 5 different classes for each school day. Discussing his assignments with a few of the school's seasoned teachers, Tom discovered that one of his predecessors quit halfway through the school year after being hit on the head with a book thrown by a student. The successor to that teacher lasted just 3 weeks. Next came one substitute, and then another, each lasting little more than 2 weeks. The current substitute had made it through her first week, and the books were still flying.

Like most new teachers, Tom wanted to succeed. But within a few weeks, the once optimistic apprentice became quite frustrated. He wrote in his journal,

> How did I get to be a teacher? Just the other day I was delivering pizzas. Now I teach Integrated Science to 150 ninth graders. They don't like to be taught. They have no desire to learn. Many are just waiting until their 16th birthday to drop out of school. I have the most difficult students. I have the least amount of experience and have just finished my training. The sensitive side of me wants to make a difference. The sensitive side of me can't sleep and gets sick at night. I don't know if I'll make it through the semester. I do not look forward to tomorrow.

Now part of the "real world of teaching," Tom began to experience anxiety and uncertainty, common feelings for many apprentices. His on-site mentor, a fellow science teacher as well as a former Teacher of the Year, offered Tom support and ideas but never brought in materials, activities, and other teacher-created items. She had only recently assumed responsibility for the school's guidance department and program, so her time was extremely limited. Without any real support from his mentor, Tom looked elsewhere.

The school's other science teachers, hardened by their years in the classroom, continued to present the same lecture-format lessons they had used for many years. They seldom involved students with science activities or experiments, just the type of learning Tom believed could motivate his ninth-grade students. His desire to use hands-on activities was hampered by the classroom's facilities, which had neither running water nor the proper equipment that a science teacher needs to be successful. Students asked Tom why he never did "neat things" like that "cool science guy" did on television each week. Rather than reacting to their chiding, the apprentice persisted and began to involve his students in various projects and activities.

Slowly, Tom began to acquire a reputation among the students that he cared for them as individuals first and as science students second. Nevertheless, he expected students to study, prepare for class, and earn their grades. His students initially were surprised when he gave them lower grades than their previous teachers. Tom believed many instructors did not expect much from students and handed out inflated grades. Some students accepted Tom's high standards and, at the second marking period, increased their grades to A's and B's.

Tom raised his image among students by taking time after school to watch some of them participate in extracurricular activities. This practice gained him support from members of the school's basketball team. Though his victories with students were small, he was willing to accept them at face value and build upon them.

Formal observations and feedback from school administrators were minimal for Tom. The principal and assistant principal each visited once during his initial 3-month period. Their feedback was positive during these visits, but they offered no suggestions on how he could improve, leaving Tom wondering why they could not offer more substantial guidance.

As Tom gained confidence, he became more involved in school events. During one staff-development activity, he met with other apprentice teachers, who exchanged their telephone numbers and e-mail addresses with him. Soon, a support network was established to share ideas, concerns, and suggestions. Most of the apprentices believed their participation in the network would be more effective than feedback from their assigned mentors.

In addition to those new allies, Tom began talking with the science department head, who offered suggestions, purchased materials, and shared ideas. As staffing plans for the next school year were being developed, the department head suddenly rearranged Tom's assignments so he could remain on staff. This step was positive, because the school district planned to assign all ninth-grade students to high schools. The assignment change meant Tom would be working with seventh and eighth graders—students who should be easier to reach and teach, he thought. Assessing his future, Tom reflected on his first few months as an apprentice and decided his successes and failures were part of growing as a teacher. Still, he knew things could have gone smoother, as he noted in his journal:

> I'll just take things one day at a time. Real progress takes time. My ninth graders achieved quite a bit and seemed to really get into learning. At least none of them threw a book at me. Even

though the administration hasn't offered me many suggestions and my mentor is mediocre, my network is growing—and next year's students should be a good challenge.

Dawn's Case

Dawn's student teaching experience at a small elementary school was exciting, exhausting, and rewarding. Her mentor carefully crafted her time to provide "consistent but retreating support," and her principal checked on her progress periodically. On most days, she left the classroom feeling challenged, yet still capable and confident. By the end of her final semester, Dawn was offered a position to teach third grade. Her childhood dream of becoming a teacher was materializing. Before she even graduated, Dawn knew where and what she would be teaching as well as who her colleagues would be. During her summer vacation, she began to review the curriculum, develop units of instruction, create bulletin boards, and organize learning centers.

A week prior to the start of school, Dawn set up her classroom. The following week, her district provided 3 days of new-teacher orientation. During the first day, between a speech about the school district's vision and learning about attendance procedures and insurance policies, all she could think about were the names on her class roster. Who were the little people behind these names? Would they like her? What were their parents like? Dawn and her fellow apprentices also attended a local university-sponsored workshop that included timely information to help new teachers prepare for their first few days. During the workshop, Dawn made the decision to register for the graduate-level course designed for apprentice teachers.

The second day of orientation was spent at the school site with her grade-level mentor. At this meeting, Dawn received a variety of materials to prepare her for the school year as well as the school's traditional "meet the teacher" afternoon. The school served an affluent suburban neighborhood and, consequently, the educated parents expected a great deal from teachers. Indeed, parents were quite vocal about wanting the "best" educators for their children. In fact, it was common for them to demand an expert teacher instead of a beginner. On the third day of new-teacher orientation, Dawn met with her grade-level team. They reviewed the schedule of special classes and discussed several curriculum ideas. The apprentice lost sleep worrying about numerous details.

The coaching Dawn received from her mentor and grade-level team helped her to begin the school year successfully. She adored her third graders and, after some effort and ongoing coaching, she had a well-managed class. Dawn found her beginning-teacher graduate course helpful, especially because she could select and reflect upon choice activities for her students. With her mentor's blessing, Dawn was able to personalize her induction program to match her needs and interests. Choosing activities encouraged Dawn to try new ideas, seek extra guidance from her mentor, and reflect more upon her practice.

By mid-October, the demands of paperwork, committee meetings, daily lesson planning, and grading were unending. By the end of the month, an exhausted Dawn attended a Saturday morning support seminar as part of her university course. She was relieved to hear comments such as, "That happened to me, too!" and "You're not alone, because I feel the same way." Exhaustion, depression, and disillusionment, she learned, were normal at this stage of her career. At the end of October, Dawn reflected,

> I have the best third-grade class. I know that last year when they hired me, the third-grade team made sure I had a class I could manage and parents who would not oppose having a first-year teacher work with their children. Some days I feel like everything comes together, and other days I feel like it's all falling apart. It definitely helps to attend new-teacher support group meetings. As we all share our problems, I know I'm not the only new teacher dealing with these issues. My mentor also offers me great ideas and a lot of support.

Defining the Apprentice Phase

The apprentice phase begins when the teacher plans, delivers, and assesses all lessons and assumes full responsibility for managing students' learning and behavior. For a few teachers, the apprentice phase begins in student teaching; for most, it will begin when they have been hired for their first teaching job and start the school year. The shift from novice to apprentice is perhaps the most complex intellectual and emotional transition on the continuum of teacher development.

Teachers are faced with a myriad of personal and professional challenges. Specifically, three areas seem to affect a majority of apprentice teachers.

Personal and professional needs. Regardless of age, level of instruction, gender, or type of preparation, apprentice teachers experience similar psychological concerns. They want to be accepted by colleagues, and they need to develop workplace friendships. In addition, they want to feel competent and secure in their job (Gold, 1992).

In the case studies, Tom and Dawn found their beginning year to be a roller coaster of contradictory emotions—simultaneously feeling excited, overwhelmed, discouraged, and rewarded. Indeed, the first year of teaching is a time for both survival and discovery (Enz & Carlile, 1998; Huberman, 1989).

Reality shock. Another common concern apprentice teachers share is dealing with the realities of full-time classroom teaching. As a student teacher, under the direct guidance of the cooperating teacher, the novice rarely makes a decision in isolation. The cooperating teacher creates the organizational framework, establishes management routines and behavioral expectations, and determines the curriculum. With a teaching "safety net" beneath them, the novice works to develop teaching strategies and management techniques. Therefore, most novices graduate with a well-deserved sense of accomplishment but an exaggerated sense of confidence and competence.

Reality shock begins as apprentice teachers, working alone, assume total responsibility and accountability for the planning, classroom management, instruction, and student assessment. Compounding matters is their underestimation of the time it takes to complete all the work (Lortie, 1975).

Teaching conditions. The apprentice teacher's ability to cope with his or her new reality is often hindered by less-than-ideal teaching conditions. Tom's experience as a first-year teacher is not uncommon. As his story illustrates, new teachers are more likely than experienced teachers to receive multiple class preparations or be assigned students who pose the greatest behavior or academic challenges. Unfortunately, because they are new, they are the least prepared to cope with these demands. Huling-Austin (1989b) summarized such abuse of apprentice teachers as "education's dirty little secret." Whether a school district's actions are a systemic sabotage or a careless indifference, the outcome, documented by numerous studies, has a devastating impact on the profession: nearly one third of all apprentice teachers leave the field before they reach the professional phase! Clearly, educators and administrators must carefully reexamine the manner in which new teachers are inducted (National Commission on Teaching and America's Future, 1996).

Threads of Continuity

Tom and Dawn are typical of most new teachers—they want to be able to teach their students and manage their classrooms successfully. Yet wanting to do a good job does not just transfer into an ability to do a good job. As apprentice teachers confront the realities of a sometimes less-than-supportive profession, it is no surprise they experience extreme emotional responses. In fact, their emotional responses are so predictable that research has identified a basic pattern through which apprentice teachers progress during their induction year.

From exhilaration to survival. Initially, apprentice teachers eagerly anticipate the beginning of the school year. They are excited to meet their students and commence their professional careers. They spend hours in their classroom preparing to teach and creating units of study. However, within the first month or so of school, apprentice teachers start to feel overwhelmed with the magnitude of their responsibility. These feelings persist as the demands of daily lesson planning, grading, parent-teacher conferences, curriculum meetings, and managing student behavior appear endless. At this point, the apprentice may become disillusioned with teaching and may begin to withdraw.

From disillusionment to rejuvenation. Apprentice teachers often have unrealistic expectations about their abilities to teach a broad range of diverse learners with unfamiliar curricula. As optimism turns into pessimism, they become frustrated and disillusioned with the teaching profession. Unfortunately, many apprentices are unwilling to share their concerns for fear their colleagues will view them as incapable. They often manage this fear by isolating themselves. Struggling alone, the apprentice feels defensive, less competent, more stressful, and withdraws further (Huling-Austin, 1989a). Fortunately, timely breaks such as traditional holidays allow these teachers to rest, think, and reflect on what they have learned and what they can do to improve. Though most apprentices return from breaks rejuvenated, some return even more discouraged and depressed, leading them to question their career choice (Murphy & Moir, 1994).

Left alone, many apprentice teachers slide deeper into withdrawal, until finally they decide to leave the field. How can the education profession prevent apprentice teachers from withdrawing?

Professional-Development Strategies

During their first year, Tom and Dawn faced many challenges. Because Dawn received comprehensive support from her school district and a local university, the challenges she confronted stimulated reflection and encouraged her professional growth. Although Tom was assigned a mentor, he received little guidance. In fact, the only support Tom received was from an informal network of other apprentice teachers, which happened almost by accident. With so many educators leaving the field, the support of new teachers is too important to leave to chance.

Most educators understand the daunting task of becoming a teacher, and most agree that new teachers need support. The type and level of support new teachers receive varies widely from state to state and district to district. Induction programs may be mandated by state departments of education as part of the standard certification process, implemented by school districts or regional offices of education as a staff-development requirement, or offered by university personnel as part of a master's program.

Principles of Effective Induction Programs

Whether the impetus for the professional development of apprentice teachers begins at the state or district level, induction programs must be (a) immediate, (b) based on the developmental needs of the apprentice teachers, and (c) comprehensively woven into the fabric of the school system.

Immediate. Effective induction programs actually begin to offer support during the hiring process (Clement, 1999). District personnel should clearly explain areas of available help for newly hired teachers during the interview process. Once the decision to hire has been made, the principal should encourage the apprentice to become acquainted with the school and community as soon as possible. Unfortunately, many apprentice teachers do not have the luxury of preparing for a specific grade level or discipline. Many first-year teachers are hired just before the start of school. Others are hired but not assigned until enrollment patterns and employment needs are determined. Then there are those teachers hired after the year begins, when schools have larger than expected enrollments.

Developmental. As a beginning psychologist, Carl Rogers (1961, p. 32) asked, "How can I treat, or care, or change this person?" Later, as his beliefs about the practice matured, he learned to ask, "How can I provide a relationship which this person may use for his own personal growth?" Likewise, induction is not something done to fix the apprentice or to make him or her fit a certain mold. Instead, good induction programs are developmental and guided by the needs of the inductee. Brock and Grady (1997, p. 42) defined developmental induction as a "sequenced set of professional growth opportunities delivered in accordance with the needs of the recipients." Good induction programs are also supportive, not evaluative. When apprentice teachers receive support from administrators, colleagues, and mentors, they are more likely to strive for effective, creative teaching (Checkley & Kelly, 1999).

Comprehensive. Tom's district relied exclusively on mentor teachers to deliver support. This practice, however, can present problems. When Tom's mentor became overcommitted, she was unable to provide the help he needed. Moreover, his school district did not offer other types of support. Effective induction programs are systemwide and multifaceted; thus, they are capable of providing a strong foundation for first-year teachers (Wasley, 1999). Dawn was fortunate to have joined a district with a comprehensive induction program. In addition, she was encouraged to enroll in a master's level university course designed to provide support to apprentice teachers.

Components of Effective Induction Programs

Comprehensive induction programs use a wide range of delivery systems and offer multiple opportunities for apprentice teachers to receive support. Dawn's district formed a partnership with a local university to provide more support services. Her district's induction program included extensive orientation prior to the start of the school year, predetermined monthly content workshops, and an assigned grade-level mentor to provide day-to-day support. The university course included choice activities designed for apprentice teachers, such as guided reflection, support-group seminars, and optional training for mentor teachers.

Effective orientations. Obviously, it is essential that apprentice teachers understand district policies and school procedures. However, too much information offered too fast is overwhelming and ultimately a waste of everyone's time. As the first day of school draws near, the apprentice's attention is focused on meeting the students and beginning the year successfully. New-teacher orientations should address the immediate needs and practical concerns of the apprentice teacher, such as learning how to access materials and the curriculum. In addition, apprentice teachers need sufficient time in their classrooms. The "nesting" process offers apprentice teachers time to plan and rehearse first-day activities (Ahr, 1998). Finally, effective orientations include time for apprentices to work with their mentors. One-on-one time allows new teachers opportunities to ask individual questions.

Effective content workshops and support seminars. Effective content workshops and support-group seminars are driven by the needs of apprentice teachers. These sessions should occur often enough for new teachers to receive information and guidance in a timely manner. However, sessions that occur too frequently (weekly) are exhausting and, therefore, not helpful.

Timely. Content workshops and support seminars must allow time for specific situations as they happen, such as preparing elementary teachers to deal with Halloween and preparing high school teachers to cope with homecoming activities. Once again, timing is essential. Information offered too far in advance of an event cannot be meaningful; information offered too close to an event will not allow sufficient time for apprentice teachers to implement suggestions. For instance, seminars about grading and distribution of report cards should be discussed a few weeks before the first grading period ends. Above all, seminar facilitators should provide the nuts-and-bolts details, because new teachers need to know "how" in addition to knowing "why" (Delgado, 1999; Scherer, 1999).

Individualized. The curriculum for content workshops and support seminars should focus on problems apprentices encounter while simultaneously helping them learn the skills of reflective teaching and professionalism (Rogers & Babinski, 1999; Veenman, 1984). Figure 3.1 presents a list of these common concerns. Just as successful teachers personalize instruction to meet the individual needs of students, so too must an induction program individualize the development of appren-

- Organizing the classroom and establishing routines
- Curriculum development and lesson planning
- Locating and selecting materials and supplies
- Classroom management and discipline
- Communicating with parents and conducting parent conferences
- Preparing for administrative evaluation
- Dealing with students' social and emotional problems
- Working with gifted and special-needs students
- Teaching strategies for grade and subject areas
- Documenting student progress
- Stress management
- Balancing personal and professional lives
- Ending the year successfully

Figure 3.1. Seminar/Workshop Topics for Apprentice Teachers

tice teachers. As Marczely (1996, p. 8) noted, "Teachers differ, not only in the professional goals they set for themselves, but also in their learning modes, stages of development, philosophies, and abilities." Individualization of support also can occur in workshops and seminars, especially when the facilitator uses small topic groups.

Interactive. Meetings for apprentice teachers should assume the tone of support groups, wherein participants share their joys and concerns to receive validation and support from one another. Facilitators succeed best when they structure portions of these seminars with activities that stimulate discussion and lead participants to reflect on their teaching, thereby encouraging growth. In addition to allowing enough time for reflection, facilitators should provide suggestions and follow-up readings for new teachers.

Mentoring

Mentoring has a long history in other professions and has become very popular in teaching. Most programs have the common goal of helping new teachers succeed, but they vary widely in their scope, philosophy, leadership, and administration, as well as who serves as mentors.

Some mentors are volunteers who teach across the school hall and see their role as simply answering questions for new teachers. Other mentors are in a more formalized role, working closely with new teachers throughout the year, attending seminars and workshops together. Some mentors are paid to work with new teachers as an "extra duty" in lieu of coaching a sport or sponsoring a school-related activity. Other mentors may be released from classroom-teaching duties to mentor a number of new teachers full-time. Many curriculum directors mentor new teachers through planned observations and peer-coaching activities. A few districts hire recently retired teachers to return as mentors.

Mentors offer the most personalized component of an induction program, serving as guide, role model, and / or friend. They help new teachers find books and materials, share workable ideas for classroom organization and management, and assist with developing new teaching strategies (Clement, 1995). Many mentors help most by simply listening to apprentices as they explain lesson plans or discuss students' behavior. As Dagenais (1996, p. 56) noted, "Mentors are expected to transmit those unwritten principles and practicalities of the educational culture to those who have taken on the challenge of helping our children learn."

Criteria for Successful Mentoring Programs

Mentors are role models for apprentice teachers, so they must be skilled, effective teachers. They must be able to promote and guide apprentices to effective teaching. The skills needed to organize a second-grade classroom and teach young children, for example, are quite different than the skills needed to teach someone else to teach the class. Just as an elementary school teacher must know about the developmental needs of young children, a mentor must address the developmental stages and needs of beginning teachers.

Mentors focus on the problems of apprentice teachers and become familiar with resources for providing help and support. As mentors learn ways to help apprentices with classroom management, teaching strategies, parental communication, and stress management, they too learn some new techniques. In fact, some veteran teachers believe mentor training is the best teacher-refresher course available.

Grade-level and subject-matter match. Being paired with a mentor who teaches the same subject and/or grade can be very helpful to a new teacher (Heller & Sindelar, 1991), because he or she can provide specific examples and resources. Being paired with a sympathetic teacher of another grade or subject level still can be helpful, especially if the mentor is a good listener and helps the apprentice reflect upon his or her classroom practices.

Time and proximity. Because a mentor needs time to support the new teacher, it is important to be in close proximity to the apprentice. Pairing a mentor with an apprentice who teaches in the same hallway and shares the same preparation time may be more effective for logistical reasons: They simply have more opportunities to talk (Enz, 1992).

Interpersonal skills. Communication skills are especially important for the mentor. He or she needs a sense of when to be direct, when to be indirect, and when to be a colleague who listens. Being a team player is, of course, another important quality, because mentors typically help apprentices fit in with other faculty members. New teachers can feel overwhelmed by the negatives heard in the teachers' lounge; they need mentors who encourage them to get to know and work with their colleagues in a professional manner.

The first years of teaching are stressful, and new teachers must learn coping mechanisms to survive in the profession. Mentors, therefore, must model not only great teaching but strong stress-management skills. In addition, they must realize apprentices need space to make mistakes and learn on their own. Sometimes a mentor has to step back, let the new teacher make unsuccessful attempts at a strategy, and wait for the apprentice to approach with a question or concern. Patience and common sense are sound mentor attributes.

Observation and coaching. Because their roles may include observation of apprentices as a way to promote effective instruction, collegial supervision and clinical supervision models (Glickman, 1985) should be taught to mentors. Learning to be a good observer is not an easy task; if observations are part of the mentoring process, then training is necessary in this area. Videotaped presentations as well as published case studies of both strong and weak classroom practices and lessons can help mentors learn about observing new teachers. Role-playing scenarios likewise aid mentors in learning to conduct pre-conference and post-conference sessions with apprentices.

Ongoing support for mentors. Mentor training should not end after one or two initial workshops and / or seminars. Like all educators, mentors need ongoing support. Throughout the school year, they can benefit from follow-up sessions to learn about new training topics, such as collegial supervision, peer coaching, or adult learning. They need opportunities to discuss ideas and solutions with fellow mentors or the group or program coordinator. When challenging questions arise about the mentor pairing—such as liability if a new teacher is not being rehired—mentors must know the answers.

Program flexibility. Some mentor pairings simply do not succeed due to conflicts in personalities or teaching philosophies. The program coordinator must then serve as an "escape valve," reassigning an apprentice to another mentor. In most cases, there is no one to blame when a pairing does not work. Usually, it is best to move on and not harm the apprentice or the mentor with dramatic reevaluations.

Recommendations for Research and Practice

To improve induction programs, colleges of education, school districts, and state agencies must work collaboratively. Colleges of education and school districts have made great strides in bridging the gap between theory and practice for novice teachers through partnerships such as professional-development schools. These sites could become centers for researching context factors that influence the induction of apprentice teachers. Is there a predictable pattern of variables more likely to favor the success or failure of apprentice teachers? Excellent models of working induction programs exist, but researchers have not examined these programs in-depth to determine why they work or under what circumstances. Why are some programs less effective than others?

Researchers might focus attention on the biology of learning to teach. Apprentice teachers experience a number of physical and psychological symptoms. Beyond attributing these problems to stress, little has been examined about this phenomenon. Researchers may also examine neural responses to determine how apprentice teachers perceive, integrate, and store information about teaching. Is the apprentice teacher's mind functioning differently or just not up to speed with the experts?

Apprentice teachers are valuable resources. We must nurture their efforts to become professionals and, hopefully, experts. How long apprentices continue and how well they develop depends, in large part, on the level of support they receive during their induction years. The philosophy of induction goes far beyond simply assisting the apprentice to survive. Comprehensive induction programs have the potential to help apprentices grow professionally by facilitating self-reflection and renewal, thus preventing persistent withdrawal.

Clearly, there were qualitative differences between Tom and Dawn's first-year teaching experiences. Tom was left to carve his own direction at nearly each step of his apprentice phase. Dawn had many factors working in her favor, including knowing the district and her grade-level curriculum. In addition, she had a chance to get to know her colleagues and had sufficient time before school began to "settle." Most important, Dawn had a formal, multifaceted induction program that offered help and support from many avenues. She had timely workshops that featured group problem-solving exercises and sharing. On top of district support, she pursued hours toward her master's program in a course designed to aid apprentices in their transition into the "real world." Dawn also was encouraged to stretch and reflect on her practice through personally selected choice activities.

Educators often speak of win-win scenarios, and an induction program can offer the best opportunities. Apprentice teachers win when they feel supported; administrators win when a beginning teacher is working effectively and efficiently in the classroom. Students learn more when their teachers are thriving, not just surviving. An added bonus is the winning rejuvenation veteran teachers feel when they serve as mentors or induction-program facilitators.

References

Ahr, T. (1998). Your classroom, your nest. *New Teacher Advocate, 6*(1), 1.

Brock, B. L., & Grady, M. L. (1997). *From first-year to first-rate: Principals guiding beginning teachers.* Thousand Oaks, CA: Corwin.

Checkley, K., & Kelly, L. (1999). Toward better teacher education: A conversation with Asa Hilliard. *Educational Leadership, 56*(8), 58–62.

Clement, M. C. (1995). Getting the most from a mentor: Message to teachers of the '90s. *New Teacher Advocate, 3*(2), 7.

Clement, M. C. (1999). *Strategies for hiring and supporting new teachers: Building the best faculty*. Lancaster, PA: Technomic.

Dagenais, R. J. (1996). Mentoring program standards. *Mentoring.* Lincolnshire, IL: Mentoring and Leadership Resource Network, Association for Supervision and Curriculum Development. ERIC ED 419 776

Delgado, M. (1999). Lifesaving 101: How a veteran teacher can help a beginner. *Educational Leadership, 56*(8), 27–29.

Enz, B. J. (1992). Guidelines for selecting mentors and creating an environment for mentoring. In T. Bey (Ed.), *Issues and aspects of mentoring* (pp. 65–78). Reston, VA: Association of Teacher Educators.

Enz, B. J., & Carlile, B. J. (1998). *Coaching the student teacher: A developmental approach.* Dubuque, IA: Kendall-Hunt.

Glickman, C. D. (1985). *Supervision of instruction: A developmental approach.* Boston: Allyn & Bacon.

Gold, Y. (1992). Burnout: A major problem for the teaching profession. *Education, 104*(3), 271–274.

Heller, M. P., & Sindelar, N. W. (1991). *Developing an effective teacher mentor program.* Bloomington, IN: Phi Delta Kappa Educational Foundation.

Huberman, M. (1989). The professional life cycle of teachers. *Teachers College Record, 91*(1), 31–57.

Huling-Austin, L. (1989a). A synthesis of research on teacher induction programs and practices. In J. Reinhartz (Ed.), *Teacher induction* (pp. 13–33). Washington, DC: National Education Association.

Huling-Austin, L. (1989b, April). *What induction can and cannot do.* Paper presented for a teacher induction conference, Arizona State University, Phoenix, AZ.

Lortie, D. C. (1975). *Schoolteacher: A sociological study.* Chicago: University of Chicago Press.

Marczely, B. (1996). *Personalizing professional growth: Staff development that works.* Thousand Oaks, CA: Corwin.

Murphy, D. S., & Moir, E. (1994). *Partnerships in education: Helping new teachers succeed.* West Lafayette, IN: Kappa Delta Pi, an International Honor Society in Education.

National Commission on Teaching and America's Future. (1996). *What matters most: Teaching for America's future.* New York: Author. ERIC ED 395 931

Rogers, C. R. (1961). *On becoming a person: A therapist's view of psychotherapy.* Boston: Houghton Mifflin.

Rogers, S. L., & Babinski, L. (1999). Breaking through isolation with new teacher groups. *Educational Leadership, 56*(8), 38–40.

Scherer, M. (1999). Knowing how and knowing why. *Review of Educational Research, 54*(2), 143–175.

Veenman, S. (1984). Perceived problems of beginning teachers. *Review of Educational Research, 54*(2), 143–178.

Wasley, P. (1999). Teaching worth celebrating. *Educational Leadership, 56*(8), 8–13.

4 The Professional Teacher

by Polly Wolfe, Diane S. Murphy, Patricia H. Phelps, and Vincent R. McGrath

Viewing the Professional Phase Through Case Study

For as long as she could remember, Sarah always wanted to be a teacher. Watching her grow from a child to an adult, her parents could see the desire and ability she possessed to lead and help others learn. A natural organizer, Sarah knew intuitively she would teach when her fifth-grade teacher selected her as the official class greeter due to her reliable, polite nature. As a teenager, she planned games and shows for the neighborhood children. When the time came for her to attend college, Sarah enrolled in a noted teacher education program and graduated with a degree and teacher certification in both elementary and special education. She applied for and was offered a teaching position working with learning-disabled students in a new elementary school with a recognized and effective inclusion policy. Her administration provided one afternoon a week for planning, a practice she believed necessary for a successful inclusion program.

The new teacher stuffed some belongings and materials into her car and drove 800 miles to a new job and culture, ready to make new friends. She established herself quickly, progressing through the novice phase of her teaching career, absorbing reality as it tempered her idealism. As an inclusion teacher, Sarah soon discovered that some colleagues treated her as an equal and a resource to be valued, but other teachers viewed her as little more than a glorified classroom aide. Some teachers arranged their Thursday afternoons to plan with her, but others were "too busy" to accommodate her and her students. Her anger usually centered on the "raw deal" her students received. Still, Sarah looked forward to collaborating with teachers on curriculum, and she especially enjoyed preparing for parent-teacher theme nights, taking time to write scripts, rehearse with the children, and work on props.

Sarah loved kids, and they noticeably reciprocated her warmth. Her conversations were punctuated with funny stories, and her tears flowed easily over their difficulties. As is typical with special-needs children, progress was sometimes slow and difficult. The incremental success of each child became her personal triumph. "I grow each time a student grows," she said. Sarah saw students integrating what she taught into their lives. She formed a special bond with her youngsters and with many of their parents, often going out of her way to make things work. On her own time, for example, she once visited several self-contained special education rooms to determine the best placement for a fragile student with communication difficulties, easing the child's transition into junior high school.

Deliberately seeking renewal, Sarah took courses in special reading methodology to help her students. As she moved out of the apprentice phase, Sarah attended professional conferences to broaden her perspective. She worked with textbook companies to pilot programs, sometimes alone, sometimes with other staff members. Despite these measures, she felt the danger of withdrawal due to staff difficulties, coupled with the immense burden of committee meetings and paperwork associated with special education. In addition, Sarah felt that her teacher training and carefully developed teaching skills were not fully used, nor was she able to pursue fully her love for curriculum development. Thus, at the end of her third year, she requested placement in a second-grade classroom. The building principal put Sarah's request on hold through most of the summer. Finally, a couple of weeks before school began, she received word that her request was accepted.

In her fourth year, Sarah exemplified the fluidity inherent within the Life Cycle of the Career Teacher model. As she began teaching in a regular classroom, she rededicated herself, working late many evenings to create learning materials. Although tired more often than not, she maintained her enthusiasm. She credited much of her success to the support she received from her new colleagues. "My team makes it work well," she noted. "They are experienced, with-it, and always updating their own curriculum. They present a united front, and, best of all, they're fun."

Sharing materials and ideas, Sarah's team worked to develop an interdisciplinary curriculum based on great ancient civilizations. Clustered in her class that year were a number of special education children. Her class was designated the inclusion room. Now it was Sarah who collaborated with the inclusion teacher to plan successfully for the special-needs students. The new inclusion teacher was treated as a valued colleague rather than as an aide.

Currently in her fifth year, Sarah is joyous about her work and thrilled with her new class. Like most professional teachers, she said she finds her deepest satisfaction from "the little notes my kids send me saying, 'You're the best teacher I ever had,' or parents saying that I really made a difference with their child. When I go to a PTA meeting, kids I had 5 years ago run up and give me hugs. They still remember when we did some fun learning activity together."

Sarah also finds renewal in professional development. Attending conferences, she takes every opportunity to present her ideas before colleagues. This past summer, she traveled to China with a fellow teacher to present her ideas on special education at an international education conference. The educators took along videos, slides, and pictures, which they used in the China portion of their curriculum.

Recognizing the importance of commitment, Sarah serves on the school district's staff-development committee as well as the mathematics, science, multicultural, and reading committees for her school. Just as she receives support from her team, she offers it to others.

When asked what keeps her in teaching, Sarah responds, "Oh, it's not the money!" She finds rewards through using her talents and love for teaching to meet the needs of her children. She sees planning as an organic, growing entity that reflects the changing needs of her students. Each year is different. She is more aware than ever of the different states of learning, understanding, and social training her children bring to the classroom. She is amazed that each year her children differ from the previous class. With changes in the classroom culture, the children bring novel problems and demands, making it a challenge to anticipate and prepare for each group of new children. Sarah knows she is a good teacher—it is reflected in the shining faces, the parents' gratitude, and the child who asks on a Friday afternoon, "Can I come back tomorrow?"

Defining the Professional Phase

Question: What about teaching makes you smile?

High school teacher's answer: "When students come back after you have had them, and they remember you or appreciate you for something you did for them."

Middle school teacher's answer: "When you make that connection with a student. It's there, and the student knows it's there."

Elementary school teacher's answer: "When my students do well on a test. When they 'get it,' that makes me feel good."

Teachers who have entered the professional phase of the career cycle focus on students and the relationships established with them. Thus, the benchmark of the professional teacher is a shift from personal needs to the needs of students. Student orientation is central to the professional phase.

The major characteristics of teachers in the professional phase can be organized in several distinct categories for practical study. The most noticeable difference between apprentice and professional teachers is increased self-confidence, which leads to commitment to the profession. Efficacy, or a belief that one is making a difference, contributes to heightened confidence as well as a greater command of pedagogy. Apprentice teachers work to develop a broader repertoire of instructional approaches; professional teachers focus on whether these strategies work with their own students (Germinario & Cram, 1998). Professional teachers devote great time and energy to modifying these approaches to fit their students' individual learning needs. Thus, this phase corresponds to Huberman's (1992) "stabilization phase" in which teachers consolidate their pedagogical repertoire.

The professional phase is uniquely characterized by continuous growth seeking. When a teacher's level of confidence increases, he or she has more emotional and mental energy, which in turn means listening to students better. Teachers receive more feedback about teaching and learning by patiently listening to their students. Responding to student feedback in a mature and insightful manner may stimulate the professional teacher to improve his or her relationship with students and experiment with approaches to teaching. In the professional phase, teachers collaborate with their students about what to learn and how to go about learning it. Supervisors no longer serve as the primary source of information during this phase.

Collegial Connections

Professional teachers are more in tune with students as well as more collegial with peers. With increased confidence, these teachers seek assistance from colleagues and become resources to others. As teachers mature, they develop networks with other teachers, both inside and outside of their own buildings. These networks commonly extend beyond their own districts. Professional teachers may establish close relationships with teachers at other schools who teach the same grade level or similar subject areas. Connections are often made at conferences. Building support networks is vital for continued growth; without them, teachers may stagnate or withdraw from the profession.

Peer interaction provides support to teachers during the professional phase. Informal conversations in hallways, at lunch, and during breaks can be helpful sources of information and inspiration. Teachers in this phase begin to share ideas and seek honest feedback. Peer coaching and techniques that involve teachers observing others teach are particularly effective. Such strategies remove the usual anxiety associated with administrative evaluations. As teachers develop trust with one another, peer coaching serves as a sound tool for improving their classroom teaching (Germinario & Cram, 1998).

Professional Issues

Question: What prompts you to make a change in your teaching?

Answer from Ron, a ninth-grade teacher: "Feeling like I'm a failure at what I've attempted to teach, or that the method I used didn't work. When I don't get my point across, I make a change."

Answer from Mark, a seventh-grade teacher: "More than anything else, it's student performance. When I see that everyone is lost, then I go back and try again."

Though the differences between these two anecdotal responses are subtle, Ron's focus contrasts with Mark's. Centered on his personal feelings, Ron has not made the transition to the level of professional teacher. Conversely, Mark has made the shift to addressing what students may be receiving through his instruction as well as how they receive it. Lasley (1998) described this transformation as "a paradigm shift," a term he borrowed from Kuhn's (1970) analysis of shifts in the physical sciences. Moving from an instructional paradigm to a learning paradigm is a distinctive mark of a maturing, caring, and competent teacher. The former orientation emphasizes methods and teacher behavior; the latter stresses learner behavior and student growth. In determining a teacher's attitude, the critical question is, "With whose performance are you most concerned?"

Fried (1995, p. 23) contended that a teacher's passion makes the greatest difference in student learning: "Passionate teachers convey their passion to novice learners, their students, by acting as partners in learning, rather than as experts in the field." Therefore, collegiality in the classroom is played out in the ways teachers approach students—that is, their psychological stance. A teacher's mental stance, according to Fried (1995), consists of what a teacher believes and how he or she acts toward students and subject matter. Characterized by respect and integrity, a teacher's relationships with students become a source of great satisfaction and pleasure.

Knowledge and the Professional Phase

What teachers know makes a difference in the classroom. As teachers move into the professional phase and feel more sure of themselves, they master certain strategies and demonstrate better command of subject content and instruction. Seeing themselves as continuous learners, they seek new knowledge about the content of their discipline, whether they teach one subject or many. With increased mastery of the theories and content within their disciplines, they learn what is most important to teach. Once they develop an effective classroom-management system, teachers have more freedom to concentrate on content and students' needs, spending less time on managing inappropriate behavior. Professional teachers can concentrate on a more intense socializing process, spending valuable time developing intellectual habits of reading and study. In addition, the professional teacher's knowledge of teaching becomes more sound. With varied reading, concentrated teaching, and patterned repetition, the young teacher slowly becomes a master of his or her material. Teaching becomes more meaningful and effective. Overall, the teacher feels confident, and his or her instruction becomes a living process.

Professional teachers' awareness reaches beyond the classroom. They understand how things work in their particular school setting—norms, expectations, history, tradition, social beliefs, and attitudes that influence teaching practices and behavior. Expectations become more clear, because these teachers have "figured out" the system. They become keen observers of the roles undertaken by the various educational players, including where the power lies, who has most of it, and how to share in getting things done. As a result, professional teachers have more mental energy to make sense of their own teaching rather than to respond blindly to school-management tasks or administrative dicta. Having learned the ropes of the classroom, these teachers begin to work effectively within larger social constructs. In turn, they are eager to share this contextual knowledge with novice and apprentice teachers.

Threads of Continuity

Despite years in the profession, the majority of teachers in schools remain in the professional phase, mastering content and management strategies and connecting with peers inside and outside their own schools. Though many will continue to reach out, reflect, and renew, many others will stagnate and withdraw. Because renewal is essential for movement along the phase continuum, it is necessary to understand factors that encourage and impede the growth of professional teachers.

Sarah, the professional teacher in the case study, sought her own avenues of renewal. She relied on her colleagues, instituted a placement change, and became professionally active outside the school. When she found no administrative support, she sought it elsewhere. Many other teachers, however, remain isolated physically and emotionally. Alone within their classrooms, some teachers hesitate to network or seek sources for renewal and support. Instead, they concentrate on the negatives in their professional lives. The education community must find ways to help both types of teachers—those who seek growth and those who are stuck in a sea of frustration. There are many avenues for engagement or reengagement, but teachers must take the initiative. Most important, administrators must provide continued and even organized support for teachers.

Reflection

Most schools allow limited time for teachers to engage in reflection and collaborative work. Professional teachers recognize the importance of reflective practice and find ways to work it into their daily routines. Some use scripts to analyze teaching situations, which Ash (1993) illustrated through questions: How might I make my classroom more inviting? Why did I conduct the lesson in such a way?

As teachers enter the professional phase, their scripts become more automatic. The habit of observation and awareness of social conditions is developed (Colton & Sparks-Langer, 1993). Indeed, engaging in reflection is valued for its own intrinsic rewards. As Osterman and Kottkamp (1993) indicated, teachers seek growth when they realize that something is "not quite right" in their own practice. To enlarge their own self-improvement goals, teachers must be encouraged and allowed to spend time in reflective activities.

Professional teachers can rely on many sources of renewal, including other teachers, staff development workshops, educational conferences, journals and other written materials, videotapes, and university courses. Teachers need access to these and other sources, and schools should take care to earmark funds for such expenditures. Giving teachers choices creates a positive climate for retaining a stable faculty and stimulating growth.

Teachers in the professional phase should be defining their own needs and creating individual growth plans. Motivation to pursue developmental activities can be modeled by senior faculty, administrators, supervisors, and expert teachers (Gordy & Phelps, 1996).

Withdrawal in the Professional Phase

Teachers in the professional phase enter withdrawal when they have little or no administrative support to renew themselves, whether through changes in their teaching practices or through university courses, travel, writing, and other means. For example, a teacher may want to create an interdisciplinary unit with other teachers, but he or she receives no support for materials or released time to plan. This lack of support may diminish a teacher's enthusiasm for an exciting project. Additionally, limited support may lead to professional-development activities that do not meet a teacher's individual needs. Such activities might be generic in nature or irrelevant to a teacher's interests. It is no surprise that teachers withdraw when they experience blocks to their growth initiatives.

A lack of collegiality among a teaching staff may also cause teachers to withdraw. If professional jealousy characterizes a teacher's relationships, then he or she is less likely to seek peer interaction. At the same time, teachers who receive little or no recognition for their special efforts, such as organizing a school presentation or serving on a curriculum-redesign committee, may withdraw from future school incentives. School support systems must include preventive mechanisms for withdrawal.

Professional teachers may become bored and stale in their classroom practices. Dull institutional routines and thoughtless habits can take a toll on teachers' educational performance. It is easy to fall behind in learning theory or changes in educational practices. Increased technological advances, however, demand that teachers find time to read, research, and discuss issues and ideas with their colleagues. It is important to find ways to prevent or alleviate teacher boredom. Ways to fight boredom often are within teachers' control as they seek renewing experiences. As Huberman (1992, p. 132) noted, "The strongest sources of career satisfaction may be potentially under our noses—in the classroom."

Finally, a mismatch between a teacher's philosophy and a school's goals may stimulate withdrawal attitudes, which in turn could lead to internal conflicts affecting performance. On the other hand, a school climate that encourages risk taking, innovation, and dialogue discourages withdrawal tendencies and increases tolerance for the rich contextual differences among teachers. Positive environments demonstrate value through teacher flexibility.

Professional-Development Strategies

During the past decade, many states have initiated programs to support new teachers in the transition from university preservice to professional teaching positions. The lessons being learned through these induction programs, as well as what is already known about teaching, serve as a knowledge base for both teachers and program developers. Thus, it is necessary to discuss issues, resources, and structures for aligning the professional phase with preservice and induction while extending opportunities for continued growth.

Much of the education literature available today emphasizes a constructivist approach to teacher and student learning. Grounded in cognitive research, constructivists support the notion that learning necessitates a change as new ideas challenge old assumptions. For educators, the process frequently means revising some views on teaching and learning before reconstructing or reinventing new ways of teaching. This learning process is continuous but especially intense during the first 5 years of teaching as apprentice teachers struggle to make sense out of multiple perspectives. State and federal school reforms coupled with advanced certification requirements further complicate a new teacher's life.

The struggles associated with this phase can be perceived in a positive or a negative light. As Piaget (1954) suggested, disequilibration is a precursor to growth, creating a necessary motivation for change. Yet change that results in renewal rather than withdrawal depends on the quality of support for learning that teachers receive as they become adjusted to their professional roles. This support can be appropriately called "professional scaffolding."

Vygotsky (1962) defined scaffolding as support that allows learners to succeed at tasks they could not otherwise do. In this era of school reform and public scrutiny, educators and policymakers who seek to build a profession by reinventing or repairing the national schoolhouse must be careful to plan and design solid structures that support the professional teacher. To inspire teachers to take on the rewarding but often risky activities of school reform, professional-development programs must bring together the goals of education and the growth needs of teachers. The structures of support and assessment offered in such programs must be research based, grounded in the mission of teaching, and carefully linked to standards for teaching and learning. Given the complexity of teaching and teacher development, programs must go beyond addressing questions of what and how to teach by acknowledging the internal questions that teachers ask as part of the reflection-and-renewal process. These programs must encourage the kind of internal analysis and dialogue that strengthen the formation of competent, caring, and qualified professional educators (Palmer, 1998).

Student Learning and Leadership

Programs to support the growth of novice and apprentice teachers must be designed to encompass the complex educational environment in which teachers work. Managing the classroom, conferring with parents, becoming a leader in the community, managing schedules, addressing discipline, and planning and delivering instruction is of great concern to the novice teacher. Developmental issues certainly continue to be raised in new teachers' minds, but by the third year many teachers focus more on student learning than their own survival needs. Their questions more and more address student needs. Over time, the content introduced to novice teachers during preservice training and apprentice development becomes more meaningfully linked to the learning status of students. Consequently, programs for developing professionals should promote an understanding of integrating curriculum and instruction with assessment of student learning.

Programs related to novice and apprentice phases should support teachers in assuming leadership roles and responsibilities. Rather than being the province of a select few, teachers should enter these roles so that isolation becomes diminished and knowledge and insights get shared with many diverse client systems. As Gehrke and Romerdahl (1997, p. 18) contend, "Leadership is every teacher's responsibility, but not at every moment." Though emphasizing leadership roles, they also addressed ways of integrating individual gifts and qualities of leadership within a teacher's daily life. The authors have broadly defined leadership to incorporate helping roles (mentors, peer coaches), linking roles (teachers who connect the school to the community), and teachers as decision-making leaders (department chairs, governing-council members, union representatives). Program developers will find Gehrke and Romerdahl's *Teacher Leaders: Making a Difference in Schools* (1997) to be a helpful resource.

Professional Competence: Linking Teacher Performance to Student Learning

Programs that scaffold professional teachers share a common objective: to help teachers promote and demonstrate a positive impact on student learning in their classrooms. Though the mission of education has always been to help students learn, the notion of assessing teacher performance in relation to student performance reflects a paradigm shift throughout the profession (Kuhn, 1970). Traditionally, professional competence has been evaluated against a checklist of prescribed teaching behaviors (Doyle, 1978); increasingly, though, educators are acknowledging that effective teaching is primarily evidenced by effective student learning (Stiggins, 1997). Such a shift requires a layered organizational response in which professional-development programs are evaluated according to their impact on classroom teachers. The resultant performance of classroom teachers is then partially measured by student achievement.

This layered response of professional accountability assumes a convergence of professional standards for teachers and essential learning requirements for students. It requires integration of knowledge about teaching with knowledge about student learning.

Administrative Action and Professional Teacher Growth

The National Board for Professional Teaching Standards (1994) certification reform compels program planners to help both teachers and administrators learn to plan and work together to enhance teacher growth. With the lack of administrative support for most professional teachers, attention must turn to program development for administrators. Administrators must learn to help professional teachers develop and carry out professional-growth plans; but they must also provide more time (through released time, substitute teachers, and teacher planning time) for teachers to reach their goals. Administrators must think about what they are doing to enhance or diminish collegiality within their buildings, districts, and subject areas. They must learn how to provide opportunities for teacher leadership and ownership. They must be educated regarding the symptoms of withdrawal, providing the scaffolding necessary for renewal. Without programmatic attention to the administrator, the professional teacher is more likely to continue struggling in isolation.

Recommendations for Research and Practice

Professional teachers develop a stance that communicates their passion to learners. This stance provides formal and informal avenues for growth, allows time for collegiality and reflection, recognizes support for mentorship training, and eliminates isolating factors. All of these elements indicate the need for strong administrative support for professional teachers. Consequently, administrators must be educated to the needs of the professional teacher along with ways to facilitate successful teacher growth.

Peer coaching and observation is one way to facilitate both the development of a passionate stance as well as collegiality. Planning time at the building and district level can encourage collegiality and content-knowledge growth. Professional organizations should become more closely aligned with schools, making themselves more accessible to teachers. Mentoring is becoming more common and should be encouraged. Administrative support must begin with the education of administrators and should be encouraged at all levels of school administration, from the school board to the principal. All stakeholders must recognize the importance of providing a cafeteria of pathways to professional growth.

Researchers can ask whether administrative support or the provision of opportunity to connect to other teachers and members of the profession makes a difference at this developmental phase. Another avenue of research might be directed at the factors isolating the professional teacher or preventing fellowship with peers. Still another area of research could concern the most effective scaffolding methods for professional teachers. Surveys of expert teachers can be conducted to discover how they found ways to grow beyond the professional stage. Particular attention must be paid to those respondents who felt withdrawal and then managed to escape it. What elements of graduate work or professional membership motivated professionals to reenter the reflection-and-renewal process? All these research areas will undoubtedly generate questions and answers that will become increasingly pertinent to the professional teacher.

As the National Commission on Teaching and America's Future (NCTAF, 1996, p. 6) emphasized, "What teachers know and can do makes the crucial difference in what children learn." The NCTAF (1996, p. 6) added, "The ways school systems organize their work makes a big difference in what teachers can accomplish. New courses, tests, and curriculum reforms can be important starting points, but they are meaningless if teachers cannot use them well." Part of the challenge for educators and policy makers is to clarify the knowledge and skills required to meet the educational challenges of the 21st century. They must also design ways to support professional teachers in fulfilling their mission as more competent, caring, and qualified teachers.

References

Ash, T. (1993). *Reflective teaching: What am I doing? Why am I doing it this way?* Regina, Saskatchewan: University of Regina. ERIC ED 360 309

Colton, A. B., & Sparks-Langer, G. M. (1993). A conceptual framework to guide the development of teacher reflection and decision making. *Journal of Teacher Education, 44*(1), 45–54.

Doyle, W. (1978). Paradigms for research on teacher effectiveness. In L. S. Shulman (Ed.), *Review of research in education,* Vol. 5 (pp. 163–198). Itasca, IL: F. E. Peacock.

Fried, R. L. (1995). *The passionate teacher: A practical guide.* Boston: Beacon.

Gehrke, N. J., & Romerdahl, N. S. (1997). *Teacher leaders: Making a difference in schools.* West Lafayette, IN: Kappa Delta Pi, an International Honor Society in Education.

Germinario, V., & Cram, H. (1998). *Change for public education.* Lancaster, PA: Technomic.

Gordy, S. H., & Phelps, P. H. (1996). Teacher educator as Ariadne. In J. Bowman & D. Fleniken (Eds.), *Modeling professional development: An Arkansas perspective* (pp. 155–163). Conway: Arkansas Association of Colleges for Teacher Education.

Huberman, M. (1992). Teacher development and instructional mastery. In A. Hargreaves & M. G. Fullan (Eds.), *Understanding teacher development* (pp. 122–142). New York: Teachers College Press.

Kuhn, T. S. (1970). *The structure of scientific revolutions.* Chicago: University of Chicago Press.

Lasley, T. J. (1998). Paradigm shifts in the classroom. *Phi Delta Kappan, 80*(1), 84–86.

National Board for Professional Teaching Standards. (1994). *What teachers should know and be able to do.* Detroit, MI: Author.

National Commission on Teaching and America's Future. (1996). *What matters most: Teaching for America's Future.* New York: Author. ERIC ED 395 931

Osterman, K. F., & Kottkamp, R. B. (1993). *Reflective practice for educators: Improving schooling through professional development.* Newbury Park, CA: Corwin.

Palmer, P. (1998). *The courage to teach.* San Francisco: Jossey-Bass.

Piaget, J. (1954). *The construction of reality in the child* (M. Cook, Trans.).

New York: Basic Books.
Stiggins, R. J. (1997). *Student-centered classroom assessment* (2nd ed.). Portland, OR: Assessment Training Institute.
Vygotsky, L. S. (1962). *Thought and language* (E. Haufmann & G. Vaker, Trans.). Cambridge: MIT Press.

5 The Expert Teacher

by Jane S. Bray, Pamela A. Kramer, and Denise LePage

Viewing the Expert Phase Through Case Study

When Emily drives into the school parking lot in the morning, at least two or three of her students are always there to greet her and carry any materials she might have with her. In the bustle before class begins, even more students hover around her desk as she prepares for the day. At the end of the school day, Emily's charges escort her back to the parking lot and bid her good-bye. The ritual will be repeated tomorrow—and the next day, and the next. It has been going on for most of the 18 years she has been teaching fourth grade.

Emily did not enter her profession until she returned to college to finish her degrees. She had completed 2 years of pharmacy school before being married and assuming the role of wife and mother. When she returned to school, she was raising four children. At that time, Emily was heavily involved in volunteer work at the local elementary school. All of her children had different educational needs, which, she believed, the local school was meeting with varying degrees of success. She decided to return to college, finish her undergraduate degree, and seek teacher certification through a master's degree. From the moment she entered the classroom as a teacher, she knew she had found her calling.

The early years were tough, but there was an immediate bond between Emily and her students. They sensed her genuine respect and love for them, returning it in full measure. She liked working with the "bad boys" the best. She knew that every boy with a chip on his shoulder behaved this way because of past experiences in school. It was a defense mechanism, and it worked. She knew that, if this pattern was left uncorrected, it could lead to more serious problems of school disengagement and potential dropout. Emily passionately believed it was her moral responsibility as a teacher to reconnect with these students and help them release the intellectual potential they all possessed. It worked! At first, her colleagues looked at her with some amusement, labeling her as just one more idealistic teacher who would soon learn that some of these children could not learn. Emily never learned this lesson.

As the years passed, Emily became known as a true child advocate. Long before the mantra "All children can learn at high levels," she believed in holding students accountable for high expectations. She routinely varied her instructional strategies, extending the amount of instructional time needed for student mastery. She understood the meaning of Gardner's (1983) theory of multiple intelligences long before he wrote the book. Students knew they could trust her, that she would not embarrass them or criticize them in subtle ways.

Now, when her district hires new teachers, Emily plays a key role in providing them with an orientation to the district. She sets the same high expectations for teacher performance that she sets for her students. After their first meeting with Emily, these new teachers are a bit scared. She plainly tells them that it is their responsibility to serve the educational needs of all children assigned to them. Unless there are extenuating circumstances, all children are expected to demonstrate mastery-level achievement of the core curriculum, and it is the newly hired teacher's responsibility to assure this success. Though careful to explain that the district has a comprehensive support system for newly hired teachers, Emily makes it clear that no teacher in the district will be recommended for tenure unless he or she exhibits the skills necessary to produce these results. They have 2½ years before a tenure decision must be made to reach this level of proficiency as classroom teachers, and she makes sure that support is provided to ensure success.

Emily exhibits this same tough student-advocacy stand when it comes to policy development, new program design, textbook adoption, parent-school involvement, and student assessment. She filters decisions about all of these issues by asking, "What does it mean for my students?" District administrators sometimes get irritated with Emily, but in their hearts they know she is right.

Gradually, Emily's sphere of influence has expanded beyond the classroom and her school. Yet she is not content to stand still in her quest for her own professional development. She is constantly driven toward self-improvement. She reads widely and deeply in her field. Her home collection of professional books would rival the local university library. Though Emily has not applied for national certification, no one doubts her ability to meet the criteria. Everyone in her community knows who she is and what she represents. She is recognized as the "pied piper" of elementary education. Her children would follow her anywhere.

Defining the Expert Phase

Teachers who reach the expert phase in the Life Cycle of the Career Teacher model represent a variety of ages and experiences. As individuals, they are impacted by both positive and negative external influences. Internally, family matters, financial concerns, and spiritual needs play important roles in their lives.

Many expert teachers develop methods for recognizing and overcoming the negative external influences on their teaching. They have reached this level of development by upholding strict standards of teaching performance and by not allowing external influences to compromise them unduly. Expert teachers continue to honor their commitment to student learning and to their own learning and teaching experiences. They continue to maintain and create relationships with colleagues, parents, and students.

Emily clearly represents the expert teacher. Expert teachers have reached the highest standards of teaching and often view themselves as members of a profession whose boundaries extend beyond the schoolhouse. As such, they often seek to meet the expectations for certification by the National Board for Professional Teaching Standards (NBPTS, 1998–1999). These expectations include the following:

- Teachers are committed to students and their learning.
- Teachers know the subjects they teach and how to teach those subjects to students.

- Teachers are responsible for managing and monitoring student learning.
- Teachers think systematically about their practice and learn from experience.
- Teachers are members of learning communities.

Emily has qualified for the Middle Childhood Generalist Certificate, taking pride in this significant professional accomplishment.

In contrast with novice teachers, who typically appear to act in a structured, inflexible manner, Berliner (1988, p. 11) categorized expert teachers as "'arational,' in that they have an intuitive grasp of a situation and seem to sense in nonanalytic, nondeliberative ways the appropriate response to make. They show fluid performance." Teachers in this phase demonstrate their expertise in the ease and automaticity of their responses to classroom situations. Henry (1994) found that expert teachers approach instructional decision making based on their own beliefs and values rather than those of colleagues, administrators, or members of the community.

Another characteristic of expert teachers is their keen recognition of diverse learners, which translates into proactive and anticipatory teaching. Emily has developed her reflective skills to assimilate student responses and adjust instruction accordingly before she delivers material and, oftentimes, as she teaches. Expert teachers are able to teach any student in any setting.

Teachers at the expert level have a global perspective of their surroundings and their students (Gollnick & Chinn, 1990). This vision enables them to create environments of mutual respect among students, colleagues, and other groups. They believe in all learners and strive to empower all students to reach their greatest potential.

Expert teachers are content in their chosen profession and confident in their ability to teach. They have technically and personally become self-assured in their roles and yet continue to strive to reach higher levels in teaching and learning. Teachers such as Emily could very well become relaxed in their professional development and still feel confident about their accomplishments. A distinguishing characteristic of expert teachers, however, is their motivation to remain engaged in the reflection-and-renewal process.

Thus, expert teachers are characterized by the continual quest for professional growth. They strive for better methods of teaching and learning and enjoy their own learning. This growth process is evident as they pursue action research in their own classrooms.

Teachers reaching the expert phase have a vast experiential base that enables them to serve as effective leaders. This leadership may be in the form of curriculum development, instructional support, new teacher induction training, and / or professional development. Instructional support teams especially benefit from the knowledge of expert teachers. Their expertise can be particularly helpful to teachers who may be struggling with meeting the needs of all students. The duration and depth of their professional experiences enable expert teachers to be effective problem solvers.

Continual growth and development are part of the expert teacher's repertoire. Novice teachers are often motivated to pursue professional development to achieve tenure or obtain salary increases. Experts are typically self-motivated to improve their teaching because of a strong commitment to the profession and a desire to be the best they can be. Many of them invest their own time and money to pursue professional-development opportunities.

Expert teachers are driven by their pursuit of new ideas. They are thrilled at the prospect of trying something original and different, thriving on opportunities to learn about current educational trends and social issues. Emily is the type of faculty member who brings new ideas to the administration for instituting change and growth in the school environment.

Finally, ethical behavior is a given with expert teachers. They strive to serve as positive role models to their students and colleagues. Expert teachers have the moral integrity to ensure that they honor their profession and themselves.

Threads of Continuity

Expert teachers view reflection as an ongoing process that includes looking back on actions and issues to determine more effective ways to carry out objectives. This approach is part of the process leading to renewal. Expert teachers usually internalize reflection. They always consider the effect their teaching has on students, positive or negative (Berliner, 1986; Darling-Hammond, Wise, & Pease, 1983). As Darling-Hammond (1998) notes,

> Expert teachers use knowledge about children and their learn-

> ing to fashion lessons that connect ideas to students' experiences. They create a wide variety of learning opportunities that make subject matter come alive for young people who learn in very different ways. They know how to support students' continuing development and motivation to achieve, while creating incremental steps that help students progress toward more complicated ideas and performances. They can diagnose sources of problems in students' learning and identify strengths on which to build. These skills make the difference between teaching that creates learning, and teaching that just marks time. (p. 7)

Teachers at the expert level pursue reflection in a collaborative manner, including dialogue, participating in focus groups or problem-solving sessions with colleagues, and serving as teacher educators in partnership situations.

As teachers evolve through the various phases of their career life cycle, differences in the way they codify their experiences—their schema—become more apparent during the reflection process (Hammrich, Bonozo, & Berliner, 1990). Apprentices often struggle with critical self-analysis due to their limited amount of classroom experience and a more structured reflection process during the novice phase. Experts rely on "procedural knowledge and instructional principles" (Hammrich et al., 1990, p. 5). Apprentices often focus on surface features of a lesson; experts focus on the underlying structure and content of a presentation.

Experts are concerned about the long-term reflection process. By comparing the present to the past, they simultaneously review experiences and incorporate new trends about the teaching-and-learning process. Expert teachers accumulate notes based on classroom observations and parental feedback. In addition, they maintain extensive files on teaching strategies. Each of these resources enables them to renew continually as professionals.

Apprentice teachers may be guided by a mentor, a principal, or other teachers. In contrast, expert teachers may be expected to function in a variety of capacities without the systematic feedback prevalent during the initial phases of their teaching careers.

Although there are numerous avenues of renewal for expert teachers, the dangers of withdrawal are still present. Experts are often frustrated by the lack of appropriate professional-development opportunities available locally. Moreover, most professional development is geared toward less-experienced teachers and seldom meets the needs of experts. Another common concern expressed is a lack of time to train, process, and develop new strategies. Fortunately, journal readings, conferences, serving on state commissions, and peer interactions are viable forms of professional-development activities in this phase. Finally, traditional sabbatical leaves provide opportunities for expert teachers to gain the quality time they need to learn and reflect on new knowledge. In addition, some experts use such time to chronicle what they have learned from these experiences. Because time is a valuable commodity for experts to revitalize their craft, it also can influence whether expert teachers move toward the distinguished phase of teaching.

Professional-Development Strategies

Expert teachers exemplify the value of lifelong learning described in the Life Cycle of the Career Teacher model. They may hold multiple degrees, including a terminal degree. Many also continue to take graduate-level courses or deliver undergraduate and graduate materials as adjunct professors. Expert teachers also contribute to the learning community by serving in formal educational positions, such as department or grade-level chairs, district representatives for community committees, and heads of curriculum-development teams.

Many times, experts take advantage of informal learning opportunities by attending workshops and conferences locally and nationally. They often are responsible for delivering and / or orchestrating formal and informal training sessions for colleagues. From these sessions, experts stay current in the field and, together with colleagues, contribute to the knowledge base. As the NBPTS (1998, p. 2) suggested, "Striving to strengthen their teaching, accomplished teachers critically examine their practice, seek to expand their repertoire, deepen their knowledge, sharpen their judgment, and adapt their teaching to new findings, ideas, and theories."

The zeal for self-improvement that expert teachers demonstrate guides them toward the distinguished-teacher level. Though they may not make this move consciously or purposely, many advance through basic self-motivation and commitment to the profession.

Experts have achieved a high level of success that enables them to be more selective about the activities they pursue. Because of the respect and the skills they possess, expert teachers can afford to be particular about job opportunities as well. For example, the expert's commitment to a professional-development school may prompt him or her to serve more effectively as a role model for novice teachers than as a mentor for apprentice teachers. Such action coincides with Berliner's (1988) view that expert teachers may be more effective as models than as coaches.

Expert teachers are visionaries who often search for "the broad picture" and become a positive force for school improvement (Gehrke & Romerdahl, 1997). Thus, leadership is a common element among experts. These teachers use what they have learned to help others within the profession. Some expert teachers use their knowledge to impact policy as they move toward the distinguished phase. As Gehrke and Romerdahl (1997, p. 1) note, "Teachers who choose to serve by leading—peer helpers, decision makers, researchers, and liaisons to the community—affirm that in doing this work they discover important contributions they can make to the larger system."

As expert teachers look toward the future, their professional role includes sharing their expertise through publications, presentations, and / or teaching. Though not all experts move toward the distinguished phase, those who do reap the benefits of their self-generated growth.

Recommendations for Research and Practice

There is still much to be learned about the development of expertise. Berliner (1986) suggested that expertise is strongly linked to context, but it is unclear how a changing context affects the teacher's expertise. Such changes in context could revolve around grade level, building, colleagues, administration, curriculum, or class population. Future research should pursue what can be done to assist teachers in transferring their expertise from one context to another. How can automaticity be transferred to a new context?

There is much to learn about this area of the educational arena. As Wolfe and Brandt (1998, p. 9) have indicated, "The recent explosion of neuroscientific research has the exciting potential to increase our understanding of teaching and learning." In addition to learning about brain functioning and its impact on learning among children, new research may also provide insight into how teachers process information at each phase in the Life Cycle of the Career Teacher model, and how that processing affects the spontaneity characteristic of expert teachers. Research along these lines would help define and validate characteristics of the expert teacher, refining the professional view and significance of educators in this phase. For example, expert teachers are not necessarily those with the most years of teaching experience (Sternberg & Horvath, 1995). Building on this data, research may lead to optimum placements of expert teachers—in the classroom and school, as teacher educators, or as community leaders. Exploring in depth the integral role that expert teachers play in the life-cycle continuum may lead to a better understanding of their expertise and how school districts can best capitalize on that expertise in various stages of the education process.

References

Berliner, D. C. (1986). In pursuit of the expert pedagogue. *Educational Researcher, 15*(6), 5–13.

Berliner, D. C. (1988, February). *The development of expertise in pedagogy.* Paper presented at the annual meeting of the American Association of Colleges for Teacher Education, New Orleans. ERIC ED 298 122

Darling-Hammond, L. (1998). Teachers and teaching: Testing policy hypotheses from a national commission report. *Educational Researcher, 27*(1), 5–15.

Darling-Hammond, L., Wise, A. E., & Pease, S. R. (1983). Teacher evaluation in the organizational context: A review of the literature. *Review of Educational Research, 53*(3), 285–328.

Gardner, H. (1983). *Frames of mind: The theory of multiple intelligences.* New York: Basic Books.

Gehrke, N. J., & Romerdahl, N. S. (1997). *Teacher leaders: Making a difference in schools.* West Lafayette, IN: Kappa Delta Pi, an International Honor Society in Education.

Gollnick, D. M., & Chinn, P. C. (1990). *Multicultural education in a pluralistic society.* New York: Merrill.

Hammrich, P. L., Bonozo, J., & Berliner, D. C. (1990). *Schema differences among expert and novice teachers in reflection about teaching.* ERIC ED 344 837

Henry, M. A. (1994, February). *Differentiating the expert and experienced teacher: Quantitative differences in instructional decision making.* Paper presented at the annual meeting of the American Association

of Colleges for Teacher Education, Chicago. ERIC ED 367 596
National Board for Professional Teaching Standards. (1998). *Guide to national board certification*. San Antonio, TX: Author.
National Board for Professional Teaching Standards. (1998–1999). *What every teacher should know*. San Antonio, TX: Author.
Sternberg, R. J., & Horvath, J. A. (1995). A prototype view of expert teaching. *Educational Researcher, 24*(6), 9–17.
Wolfe, P., & Brandt, R. (1998). What do we know from brain research? *Educational Leadership, 56*(3), 8–13.

The Distinguished Teacher 6

by Billie J. Enz, Kathleen R. Weber, and Ruth D. Campopiano

Viewing the Distinguished Phase Through Case Study

Kathy is a leader in her school. During her 17-year career, she has served on and chaired dozens of school, district, and teacher-association committees. Over the years, her contributions have benefited students and teachers immensely. With the encouragement and support of her building administrator, Kathy has presented workshops at district, state, and national conferences. She consistently participates in a broad range of professional-development workshops.

One year, during a professional-association meeting, Kathy learned about a new program called the National Board Certification for educators. Intrigued by the opportunities for self-development and personal-professional reflection that the certification process offered, she decided to pursue it. As with most of her commitments, Kathy succeeded, becoming the first teacher in her state to receive National Board Certification. "This experience transformed me from a good teacher to a very good teacher," she commented about the certification process. Being named as her state's teacher of the year also boosted her confidence.

Hoping to share her experience with colleagues and other educators, Kathy worked with a university faculty member to develop a mentor program as well as a course for teachers to prepare for their own National Board Certification. She continues to expand her influence on the profession by teaching a site-based undergraduate methods course.

Because Kathy enjoys challenging herself, it is natural that she became an active grant writer. She began to write grants to help her school obtain funds for special learning projects. During her review of the many grants available, she noticed that some offered substantial monetary awards, including her favorites, the Christa McAuliffe Fellowship and Disney's American Teacher Award. These sources were excellent means to provide funds for Kathy's technological endeavors in the district. Her motivation, however, came from her school's need for up-to-date equipment to provide greater benefits for students.

Kathy is passionate about teaching. She uses puppetry to teach concepts to elementary students and has established a reputation for this unique and imaginative methodology. Kathy exudes enthusiasm and passion for teaching. "This career," she notes, "is all-consuming. It is always on my mind." She views herself as "part of the flock," but her recognition as a distinguished teacher allows Kathy to be a vocal advocate for a variety of causes. She is both surprised and pleased when asked to share her opinion and advice. Kathy has a quest to promote the profession. "Most schools are great resources of knowledge and goodness," she says, "especially when teachers take the time to learn from and grow with other teachers."

Kathy is a distinguished teacher. Her commitment to students and teaching, as well as her consistent leadership at local, district, and state levels illustrate the impact she makes on the profession.

Defining the Distinguished Phase

Scholars have written about expert teachers (Berliner, 1986; Sabers, Cushing, & Berliner, 1991), yet few have written about distinguished educators in a systematic way, beyond case studies or biographies. The teaching profession has traditionally limited the definition of distinguished educators to those individuals who have received formal recognition as Milken Teacher Award winners, Disney's American Teachers Award winners, National State Teachers of the Year (NSTOY), and Golden Apple Fellows. If "distinguished teacher" is merely a title bestowed upon a small subset of expert teachers, however, then the number of distinguished teachers depends on the limited opportunities experts have for formal recognition. On the other hand, if becoming a distinguished educator is a phase of teacher development, how is it any different than the expert phase? The lack of research about distinguished educators makes this question difficult to answer. The perception that expertise is the terminal level of teaching competence complicates the issue; thus, the category of expert teacher may be too broad.

The distinguished educator may possess more than extraordinary teaching skills. Educators like Kathy, for example, "exceed everyone's definition of exemplary teachers" (Steffy & Wolfe, 1997, p. 18–19). If the emphasis of expertise is placed solely on teaching skill, then the unique dispositions and attitudes of the distinguished educator may be overshadowed.

Threads of Continuity

To gauge what differentiates the distinguished teacher from the expert, 29 NSTOY members were asked to complete an open-ended survey. In all, 26 completed and returned the survey; 12 respondents were primary teachers, and 14 taught in middle or secondary schools. The 26 respondents surveyed had, on average, 23 years of teaching experience, with a range of 8 to 35 years. They responded to three questions:

- What differentiates an expert teacher from a distinguished teacher?
- What activities or functions help to renew your enthusiasm for teaching?
- What might cause you to withdraw from the teaching profession?

Though all 26 NSTOY members responded to the survey independently, their answers were remarkably similar. Following is a summary, with excerpted quotes from their written comments.

Differentiating the Expert Teacher From the Distinguished Teacher

NSTOY members considered experts to be incredibly competent teachers, committed to their students and the profession. Most of the

NSTOY members viewed themselves as experts but identified key features they believe differentiate expert teachers from distinguished educators: passion, leadership, and impact.

Passion

NSTOY members often described distinguished teachers as being passionate about their chosen profession. As one respondent noted, "The distinguished teacher is marked by a 'missionary zeal' that transcends the boundaries of career and teaching assignments." As another said, "Distinguished teachers seem to have a vision and mission that pervades their life. Their commitment, dedication, and enthusiasm for teaching directs their days and nights." This passion is directed toward their students first: "The children's futures are the focus of every action, because they believe every child is a unique, valuable person, capable of success."

Perhaps because they viewed students as the central focus of their efforts, several NSTOY members suggested that distinguished teachers were more likely to build the curriculum around the needs and interests of their students than to fit the children into the demands of the curriculum. Their passion also translates into determined action. As one NSTOY member noted, "Distinguished teachers will not be deterred from doing whatever it takes to accomplish the goals set by their students. They seek untapped resources and are not defeated by bureaucratic red tape."

Leadership

NSTOY members described distinguished teachers as self-assured leaders and risk takers who share their knowledge with peers, new professionals, the wider educational community, and local, state, and national politicians. Many of the NSTOY members who responded to the survey held positions of leadership in national education organizations. As one respondent indicated, "Distinguished teachers are seen and see themselves as responsible for sharing their experiences, knowledge, opinions, advice, and support." As another noted, "Distinguished teachers are self-assured born leaders and self-starters extraordinaire. They are movers and shakers and move easily in political, business, and teacher circles."

Impact

The combination of passion and leadership leads to the attribute of distinguished teachers described most frequently by NSTOY members: impact. These teachers defined their role as going beyond the walls of the classroom. Respondents suggested that distinguished teachers have vision and an acknowledged voice that influences the instructional direction of their schools, districts, states, and, in many cases, the nation: "Distinguished teachers have a broad involvement in education. They have a viewpoint that includes issues in their field beyond the school, district, and state."

Distinguished teachers are often the main force in changing the culture of schools; for example, they provide additional tutorial services for students, such as establishing academic clubs. Caring about children, their families, and the community, as well as a deep concern for the quality of a child's home life, further defines this high-impact teacher. As one respondent indicated, "Distinguished teachers impact children's lives beyond the walls of the classroom, beyond instruction. They consider the needs of the whole child and take deliberate actions to ensure that children come to school ready to learn, whether that means new glasses or hearing aids or even appropriate school clothes."

Erikson's (1982) work may help explain the psychological motivation behind the beliefs and actions of distinguished teachers. He defined, in broad, bipolar terms, the psychosocial terms of adulthood as generativity versus stagnation. All teachers who successfully progress through the career life cycle are generative. However, in their written comments and interviews, these distinguished teachers voiced what Erikson called an urgent commitment to care. These distinguished teachers demonstrated a level of commitment that stretched beyond their own classrooms; they felt a need to improve the quality of life for all. This passion and initiative reflected a moral dimension that Kohlberg (1984) called the universal ethical principal orientation.

Like Kathy, NSTOY members were compelled to respond to the needs of others and worked to change the social system. These actions suggest what Noddings (1993) described as the ethics of caring. Many of the NSTOY members' comments suggested that they viewed the role of teacher and the act of teaching as giving profound meaning to their lives.

Renewing Enthusiasm for Teaching

NSTOY members cited various sources of renewal. Themes commonly revolved around five sources: intellectual stimulation, collegial interactions, shared knowledge, changes and challenges, and student interactions.

Intellectual Stimulation

Distinguished teachers attend and present at national, state, and local professional conferences. The opportunity to learn and share new ideas energizes and motivates them. As one NSTOY noted, "Networking and time spent with other professionals gives me time to plan, think, and reflect about old and new ideas."

Collegial Interactions

Distinguished teachers found it important to work with other colleagues. In particular, many of the NSTOY members spend time with other distinguished teachers, as one NSTOY's comments illustrate: "Being around other distinguished teachers is energizing. I find their enthusiasm and self-motivation is 'electric,' and I am always 'recharged' after being with them."

Shared Knowledge

Like the professional and the expert, distinguished teachers enjoyed working with preservice and beginning teachers. It stimulated reflection and provided unique opportunities to teach and reflect on teaching. As one respondent noted, "Working with new teachers is exciting. I enjoy watching them learn and become more confident. I also learn new ideas from my student teachers, and I love to share information and ideas. It sharpens and improves my own skill."

Changes and Challenges

Distinguished teachers welcome opportunities for growth. They mentioned that attaining a higher degree, seeking National Board Certification, conducting classroom research, piloting a new curriculum, or changing grade level offers intrinsic motivation for them. Distinguished teachers enjoyed changing roles, adding that conducting inservice sessions for colleagues or teaching methods courses for the university was, as one exclaimed, "highly demanding, but exciting!" These distinguished teachers had confidence and sought ways to expand their knowledge and skill.

Student Interactions

Distinguished educators identified their students as the most consistent and important source of professional renewal. At a basic level, students' needs and interests motivated these teachers. Student responses and successes inspired them. Previous students were also a source of renewal. One NSTOY member, for example, said she was motivated when she "got responses from students and parents that show you that your efforts have made a difference in their lives." As another NSTOY member noted, "Meeting the needs of my students is motivating. Each year brings new faces and a new classroom of challenges that stimulate me."

Distinguished Teacher Withdrawal

NSTOY members were less consistent in their responses regarding the events that could cause them to withdraw from their profession. Though two members could not imagine anything that could cause them to "give less than their best," most members wrote about two or three issues that could cause them to question their place in the profession. Among these, personal crisis, professional image, and unresponsive administration were most often cited.

Personal Crisis

NSTOY members identified physical health or family crisis as a potential reason for withdrawal from their professional obligations. Many supported both the older generation (their parents) and younger generation (their children and grandchildren). As one respondent acknowledged, "It would be difficult to continue to give your 'all' when you are seriously ill or members of your family (parents or children) need you."

Professional Image

Some NSTOY members discussed the powerful impact of negative media attention. The focus on the negative has a serious demoralizing effect on teachers. One respondent summarized the views of a number of NSTOY members: "I have found the constant media disparagement of schools and the efforts of those in the public school very painful. I know many teachers who have retired early because they are tired of working 12-hour days to hear on that day's news what a lousy job they are doing."

A number of NSTOY members felt that school board members and legislators were often "clueless about what teachers do." Several mentioned they were tired of politicians "blaming the problems of society on the public schools." As one respondent commented, "Politicians think anyone can teach or believe they have all the answers when they have never worked one day within the public school system. This attitude is demeaning to all teachers."

Unresponsive Administration

The greatest problem nearly all NSTOY members identified was unresponsive administrators. Building principals who did not encourage professional development for teachers and did not put students' needs first were especially troubling. As one NSTOY member indicated, "Principals can impact a school in wonderful or horrible ways. They can support or inhibit new programs for children and teachers." Another respondent noted, "Principals can empower teachers or they can undermine teachers. If principals feel their job is to control the school, then there is a problem. Good principals encourage teachers to be in control."

Professional-Development Strategies

Distinguished teachers consistently have highly complex mental schemas for interpreting students' needs, classroom interactions, curriculum organization, and presentation. They reflect upon their instructional practices and classroom interactions. They seek opportunities to grow and integrate new knowledge into their classrooms. They need challenges to keep them abreast of their profession.

Opportunities to Learn

Most of the NSTOY members commented on the importance of continued professional development. Though these educators strive to continue to improve their practice, they need support from administrators. The NSTOY members argued that distinguished teachers need intellectual stimulation. Most of them acknowledge the important role professional conferences play in their careers. Districts must provide funds for distinguished educators to attend professional conferences. Information distinguished educators gather at these conferences is then easily shared with colleagues.

Time to Reflect

Nearly all of the NSTOY members thought time was a necessary requirement for reflection and renewal. They wanted time to work with peers and new teachers; they valued time to think about the changes in their field and their students' needs. In the public schools, time is a precious, difficult commodity to obtain. The very nature of school makes it difficult for teachers to attend conferences. Likewise, the organization of the school day places constraints on time for colleagues to discuss school matters.

Professional Challenges

Distinguished teachers need professional challenges. They enjoy coaching student teachers and helping adult learners. They also enjoy teaching methods courses and developing curriculum and training models for peers. They profit from developing new methods of instruction or conducting classroom research. Changes in roles and responsibilities are stimulating and invigorating.

Recommendations for Research and Practice

Distinguished and expert teachers share a number of common characteristics. Both are motivated, examine their practices, and strive to strengthen their teaching. The 26 NSTOY members who responded to the survey identified some differences that they perceived. Though they acknowledged the importance of their titles, they believed their passion, leadership, and influence truly differentiated them from expert teachers. The NSTOY members believed that these qualities, in addition to their teaching skills, ultimately led to the recognition they had received. Because the survey was small and the research sparse, a firm conclusion cannot be reached.

The knowledge base about gifted professionals must be expanded. This study suggests that distinguished teachers reach beyond the bounds of expert teachers. Their passion, leadership, and impact on the profession place them in the expert phase of teacher development. Additional research could examine distinguished teachers reflecting on their work and how it differs from experts' reflection practices. Addressing withdrawal, researchers could focus on motivating teachers throughout the career cycle.

The distinguished teachers surveyed for this study have many leadership qualities. How do they demonstrate leadership within the school setting? How can schools use these skilled leaders without losing their talents as classroom teachers? Could these individuals have more flexible schedules to enable them to work with other teachers?

Distinguished teachers are exemplars of personal and professional quality. They demonstrate the highest degree of competence and passion about their students. They dignify the teaching profession. They are proactive educators, automatically reflecting on their teaching practice and constantly challenging themselves to grow. Their talents and interpersonal skills inspire colleagues. They are willing to assume the obligations of leadership. Their influence extends beyond the classroom to highlight the wonders of education and the challenges of teaching today and tomorrow.

References

Berliner, D. C. (1986). In pursuit of the expert pedagogue. *Educational Researcher, 15*(7), 5–13.

Erikson, E. H. (1982). *The life-cycle completed: A review.* New York: Norton.

Kohlberg, L. (1984). *Essays on moral development,* Vol. 2. New York: Harper & Row.

Noddings, N. (1993). Caring: A feminist perspective. In K. A. Strike and P. L. Ternasky (Eds.), *Ethics for professionals in education: Perspectives for preparation and practice* (pp. 43–53). New York: Teachers College Press.

Sabers, D. S., Cushing, K., & Berliner, D. C. (1991). Differences among teachers in a task characterized by simultaneity, multidimensionality, and immediacy. *American Education Research Journal, 28*(1), 63–88.

Steffy, B. E., & Wolfe, M. P. (1997). *The life cycle of the career teacher: Maintaining excellence for a lifetime*. West Lafayette, IN: Kappa Delta Pi, an International Honor Society in Education.

7 The Emeritus Teacher

by Raymond J. Dagenais, Betty E. Steffy, and Billie J. Enz

Viewing the Emeritus Phase Through Case Study

Mary, Clara, and Harry are part of what they call "the gray brigade." They met 6 years ago at a Retired Teachers Association meeting, warmed up to one another immediately, and began a lasting friendship. The trio has reached the emeritus phase of the Life Cycle of the Career Teacher model. They cared passionately about their profession when they were teachers, and that passion continues today. All are actively involved in helping schools improve and children succeed. Each of them goes about this quest in a very different way. Mary is a political activist well known in the halls of the state legislature. Clara, who volunteers in a fourth-grade classroom at a neighborhood school, knows how to provide underachieving students with the gift of resilience. Harry is known for achieving a 100 % success rate in mentoring teachers through the apprentice phase. All of these emeritus teachers continue to make significant contributions to the field of teaching, yet on their own terms and in their own ways.

For Mary, Clara, and Harry, teaching is not work. It was—and still is—a chosen lifestyle they will continue to pursue as long as their health and energy levels permit. Though they are pursuing very different paths, each feels rewarded.

Mary gets a "high" from seeing her ideas reflected in the language of proposed new legislation. She knows every member of the State Education Subcommittee on a first-name basis. When a new member is appointed to the committee, she makes it her business to develop a personal profile of the legislator, set up an appointment with him or her, and provide the individual with historical information about the structure of education at the state level. She has a reputation for being savvy, direct, and knowledgeable about national trends in education. Mary has a strong education advocacy network statewide that she can activate quickly. When she speaks, legislators and aides from the governor's office listen. Rumor has it that she has been part of closed-door discussions when delicate educational issues were on the agenda. Mary knows she is influential, yet her guiding principle is always the same: "How will an action, statute, or regulation enable more children to meet high academic expectations, develop a sense of worth, become resilient, and internalize a personal passion for knowledge?"

Clara is 75 years old and has been retired for 13 years. For the past 10 years she has been a fixture at a local elementary school, arriving each day at 7:30 A.M. and staying until well after the children have gone home. Not only does every student in the school know Clara, every parent and teacher knows her too. She has touched every one of their lives in some special way. Though the fourth-grade class is her home base, Clara goes wherever the school needs her most. She particularly bonds with fourth-grade boys just when they develop reputations for misbehaving. She seeks them out and spends informal time with them—chatting before school, eating with them in the cafeteria, and just "hanging out." Kids listen to her because she listens to them. She has become a second parent to dozens of children who lack a vital anchor in their lives.

Though age is taking its toll on Clara, her step stays lively and a twinkle remains in her eye. Clara keeps up on all the latest crazes, TV shows, and computer games. She has a knack for using examples from the current kid culture to serve as models for long-term goals. The district board of education recently presented her a special volunteer-service award. Clara says she will stay with the school as long as she is wanted. The children, teachers, and parents hope there are many years ahead for the wonderful gift she brings to their lives.

As a teenager, Harry enjoyed teaching children how to play sports. When he became a Little League baseball coach, he knew his profession should be that of a teacher. Upon completing his undergraduate teacher education program, Harry applied for a position in a school district that needed male teachers for coaching jobs as well. With a healthy interest in the outdoors, he worked with Boy Scouts, church groups, and other organizations. All these things helped Harry land a job as a fifth-grade teacher.

Like most new teachers, Harry was not confident and comfortable. The novice thought he could answer parents' questions adequately but felt some parents did not accept him due to his lack of experience. After a few years of success with students, Harry gained confidence in his teaching abilities, and acceptance increased in the eyes of parents, administrators, and fellow teachers as he grew professionally.

Harry utilized his diverse extracurricular interests and activities to make his classroom "come alive." At the midpoint of his teaching career, he began his formal studies of outdoor education, involving students in exploring the environment and integrating this learning into other units. This innovative work demanded commitment and energy, yet it also required a degree of trust from the administration. Harry's supervisors knew that he would address "the basics" by using an outdoor education approach. The students always performed well on a variety of assessment measures. Nominated for "Teacher of the Year," Harry was honored his peers chose him for the award, knowing that, in accepting it, he was representing a deserving group of other teachers. He perceived the award as a statement of acceptance and an acknowledgement of his desire to excel.

Growth in expertise and confidence opened other teaching opportunities. Harry began to mentor novice teachers for a local university. During the latter part of his career, he worked intensively with 16 student teachers. To ensure their success, Harry slowly phased them into the classroom work. Students first would observe, then teach a lesson on spelling or reading. Eventually, they would assume the entire class load to gain experience with all the teaching responsibilities. All 16 of Harry's protégés landed teaching positions. Interacting with them helped him reflect upon and improve his own teaching.

Most aspiring teachers were receptive to Harry's mentoring approach. Along with the strategy of easing them into the teaching role, he believed they could use small failures as focal points for reflection, renewal, and growth. Having experienced his share of failure, he understood the necessity of learning from mistakes. Harry credits several great role models, coaches, teachers, and peers who helped him learn from such experiences. These were people who provided support when he needed assistance.

After his formal retirement, Harry decided to expand his involvement with novice and apprentice teachers. He worked with the local university to write a grant to provide transition services to apprentice teachers through the induction period. The program has been so successful in providing support for newly hired teachers that the state legislature is considering providing funds for other districts to implement the model. All of the teachers involved in his program have continued in their positions as teachers. After 32 years in the teaching profession, Harry has found a niche that gives him almost more pleasure than when he was a regular classroom teacher. He has discovered how to minimize the impact of withdrawal during the apprentice phase and enable these new teachers to continue and expand the reflection-renewal-growth process.

Defining the Emeritus Phase

As we mentioned in Chapter 1, those educators who retire after a lifetime of teaching during which they achieved the skills of an expert or distinguished teacher deserve society's thanks and praise. Their efforts have prepared the way for thousands of students to enter the world of work and adulthood ready and inspired.

For some teachers, however, retiring is not enough. Emeritus teachers are those who have formally retired but, due to their expertise and devotion, continue to be active and involved contributors to the profession (Steffy & Wolfe, 1997). Individuals entering the emeritus phase make excellent candidates for mentoring the next generation of teachers. Retirement from the teaching profession is the most clearly defined transition in the Life Cycle of the Career Teacher model, with the exception of the important step novice teachers take when they accept responsibility for their own classrooms. United States Secretary of Education Richard W. Riley (in Watson, 1998) has warned that, in the next decade, public schools will need to hire 2.2 million teachers to keep pace with rising enrollments and to replace a generation of retiring teachers. This projection has important implications for teachers already in retirement, especially those at the emeritus level.

In her book *New Passages—Mapping Your Life Across Time*, Gail

Sheehy (1995, p. 373) asks, "What association first comes to your mind when you hear the word retirement? Reward? Release? Being put out to pasture?" Retirement and the emeritus phase can take on many different meanings and definitions. Moreover, it is usually planned during an entire career. Emeritus teachers choose to remain active contributors to the profession, even in retirement. Though retirement is generally not a spur-of-the-moment decision, factors such as age, health, finances, and family status also influence this decision.

The question of financial security is usually a major consideration in deciding when to retire. Strategies and mechanisms such as personal-savings plans and pension funds provide the financial resources when employment income is terminated. If attention is not paid to the issue of financial security far in advance, a teacher's options may be severely limited. Financial insecurity could lead even distinguished teachers into complacency and withdrawal.

People generally do not retire in their twenties or thirties. Arriving at the conclusion that "all that could be accomplished in the profession has been successfully achieved" requires the wisdom and insight of experience. Aging also prompts health considerations. Declining health is a condition that can weigh heavily on a teacher, perhaps prompting a decision to retire at an earlier age.

Familial relationships can also affect an individual's retirement. Spouses take on new interests or change careers. Once their formal education has been completed, children leave home to begin their own lives. These events offer opportunities to reflect upon life changes and renew one's commitment to teaching. During such times, career teachers can develop new interests and opportunities, such as working with younger teachers in "helping" roles. The emeritus teacher shares the same conditions facing any retirees; but he or she chooses to stay active and involved in teaching.

Threads of Continuity

Mary, Clara, and Harry have successfully progressed into the emeritus phase. Having invested many years in the profession, achieving a high level of expertise and wisdom, and perhaps achieving expert or distinguished status, these teachers are clearly special in many ways. Yet, like others who retire from teaching, they reflect on nurturing and supporting family members, developing vital networks of friends and colleagues, establishing a sound personal finance plan, and exploring new avocations. As a teacher begins to reflect about retirement, the direction a teacher takes may depend upon what phase of the life cycle has been achieved prior to retirement. The strength of factors leading to withdrawal can propel a teacher to reject the emeritus phase. Continued commitment to reflection, renewal, and growth can naturally lead the teacher to the emeritus life-cycle phase. Teachers who have consistently employed the reflection-renewal-growth process throughout their career appear more likely to continue contributing to their profession in some unique capacity. If individuals reach a retirement decision in withdrawal, they most likely will not choose to enter the emeritus phase.

Emeritus teachers are willing to continue helping others while staying interested in their own learning. This commitment is the underpinning of emeritus status. In no other phase do teachers have as many growth options. Emeritus teachers can choose pathways that build upon their expertise and experience.

Volunteering at the local library to help people learn to read, tutoring students in mathematics, coaching soccer or Little League baseball, training individuals in the use of technology, or mentoring novice and apprentice teachers—all are possibilities for emeritus teachers. Renewal occurs when one "commits" to assuming the responsibility for helping others.

Professional-Development Strategies

Emeritus teachers may be invited to teach methods classes at a local university and share their wisdom and time-tested teaching practices. Students relate well to veteran teachers who continue to reflect, renew, and grow. Additional opportunities include acting as a supervisor of student teaching. Student teachers benefit greatly from the sage advice and feedback of an emeritus teacher who also can play a part in the induction of new teachers into the profession. In this role, the emeritus teacher can reflect on the complete career life cycle and prepare new teachers to anticipate and cope with unexpected challenges.

Teachers reaching the emeritus phase also become tutors for young students needing special learning assistance. Emeritus teachers may choose to tutor individuals or small groups of students so they can maintain a level of academic achievement perhaps impossible without this intervention.

Recommendations for Research and Practice

The cadre of emeritus teachers has been largely underutilized as a valuable resource. Research studies could supply valuable information that predicts the impact of emeritus teachers. For example, which state-mandated teacher-induction mentoring programs have successfully capitalized on the skills and experience of emeritus teachers? This type of research should ensure that the ultimate purpose of professional development is less to implement a specific innovation or policy and more to create habits and structures that make continuous learning a valued and endemic part of the school culture (Fullan & Stiegelbauer, 1991).

Recent research conclusions also suggest possibilities for further study on this issue. Dagenais (1990) found that strong matches between mentor and protégé were positively correlated with successful mentoring experiences. Further research could identify what characteristics were most important in successful matches between emeritus teachers and novices. This study could generate information crucial to the implementation of successful mentoring experiences for these individuals.

New teachers have reported that the time they spent with their mentors was not as great as they expected (Dagenais, 1990). Research could document the amount of time emeritus teachers spend with teachers in the apprentice phase and the quality or usefulness of the interaction. This type of study could determine how time was spent, what concerns were discussed, and what information was shared, providing guidance for emeritus teachers considering a mentoring role.

Emeritus teachers have many choices to make concerning how they will continue to serve the profession. Like Clara and Harry, some emeritus teachers may choose to continue to work with children. Some may choose to write journal articles, books, or other types of print materials. Some may be technologically inclined and participate in Internet communication. Some may lead or direct university programs designed to help new teachers grow. Like Mary, some may decide to become politically active for the benefit of students.

Drawing on the work of Erikson (1968), Palmer (1998, p. 49) noted that renewal "suggests the endless emergence of the generations, with its implied imperative that the elders look back toward the young and help them find a future that the elders will not see." The emeritus teacher has a role in ensuring that teacher development follows such energizing pathways.

References

Dagenais, R. J. (1990). *A study of selected ability, physical, and psychological variables and the achievement of a successful mentoring experience.* Unpublished doctoral dissertation, Northern Illinois University, DeKalb, IL.

Erikson, E. H. (1968). *Identity, youth, and crisis.* New York: W. W. Norton.

Fullan, M. G., & Stiegelbauer, S. (1991). *The new meaning of educational change.* New York: Teachers College Press.

Palmer, P. J. (1998). *The courage to teach: Exploring the inner landscape of a teacher's life.* San Francisco: Jossey-Bass.

Sheehy, G. (1995). *New passages—Mapping your life across time.* New York: Ballantine.

Steffy, B. E., & Wolfe, M. P. (1997). *The life cycle of the career teacher: Maintaining excellence for a lifetime.* West Lafayette, IN: Kappa Delta Pi, an International Honor Society in Education.

Watson. R. (1998). The need for more schoolteachers in science and math: How colleges can help. *The Chronicle of Higher Education, 45*(6), p. B9.

8 Applying the Life Cycle of the Career Teacher Model

by Suzanne H. Pasch, Michael P. Wolfe, Betty E. Steffy, and Billie J. Enz

With this book, we have tried to characterize and encourage the lifelong development of career teachers through a reflection-and-renewal process that leads to continuous growth. The opening chapter describes the Life Cycle of the Career Teacher model. This closing chapter describes how to apply the model to encourage growth throughout the career.

Beginning with the presentation of the Life Cycle of the Career Teacher model and continuing with the elaboration of each of its phases in distinct chapters, we have presented a developmental continuum that describes movement across its phases as a means for teachers to stay vital, informed, and purposeful. The model allows teachers to maintain excellence for the benefit of all learners across a lifetime in the profession. Repeatedly, the teachers and teacher educators who have written this book have advanced the belief, grounded in theory, research, and practice, that all teachers can reach a standard of excellence in the first 5 years of teaching. With the appropriate support, teachers can continue to enhance their abilities throughout their careers, using reflection and renewal as the mechanism to propel personal and professional growth.

In the discussion of each phase of the Life Cycle of the Career Teacher model, the contributors to this book have helped us underscore issues and characteristics that make each phase distinct, introduce threads of continuity and an overall vision of excellent teaching that connect each phase to those that precede and follow it, and provide strategies for professional development and for research and practice that emerge from each unique phase. In this final chapter, we focus holistically, as we did in the first chapter, on the Life Cycle of the Career Teacher model to

- Present implications and recommendations across phases for the development of individual teachers and the teaching profession
- Focus on the relationships and interactions among teachers and other members of the learning community that influence positively the reflection-and-renewal process
- Challenge us, as members of a profession, to test and implement this model that views ensuring the development of its practitioners as one of the profession's main responsibilities

Implications and Recommendations for Lifelong Development of Teachers

The key to maintaining excellence throughout the teaching career lies in one's ability to continue to grow as a professional. The reflection-and-renewal process, within a strong learning community and in a positive social context, feeds this growth directly.

Maintaining the Reflection-and-Renewal Process

The reflection-and-renewal process both impels development across the phases and serves as an intervention against withdrawal. Though the growth process changes—over time, across individuals, and through the phases—the processes of reflection and renewal remain constant and operate as the mechanism through which growth occurs.

The value of the Life Cycle of the Career Teacher model lies in its ability to influence practice in a positive direction. To apply the model as a guide for the development of teachers, though, developing professionals must learn about the model, its phases, and its growth process in the workplace. Then, the Life Cycle of the Career Teacher model and its reflection-and-renewal process may be used as a framework to guide practice.

Specifically, the model provides

1. *A means for assuring that teachers grow professionally.* The model specifies an entry and exit point to career development and delineates phases that provide a direction for growth between those points. Through reflection and renewal, teachers remain current, competent, caring, and enthusiastic about what they do at each phase of professional development.

2. *A framework for designing professional-development activities to support growth.* Recognition of the characteristics of the career phases can lead directly to professional growth activities that reflect different levels of development among teachers and address different needs they have across the career.

3. *A process that must be nurtured and encouraged for growth to occur.* Movement from phase to phase does not occur automatically, functioning instead in the supportive relationships and recognition of the role that the individual within a social context plays in promoting reflection and renewal.

4. *A new vision of the profession as playing a powerful role in its own development.* Within our schools lies a wealth of intergenerational, interrelated expertise for supporting growth just waiting to be tapped. Applying the Life Cycle of the Career Teacher model, with its reliance on a reflection-and-renewal process as the means to move from phase to phase, implies that we accept responsibility for creating workplaces in which teachers can learn and grow across the career and for using the resources of teachers to promote that growth.

For professional development to progress across the phases of the life-cycle model in these ways, however, teachers must be provided with opportunities and time to engage continually in the reflection-and-renewal process. School districts must address this crucial need.

Supporting the Development of Teachers as Individuals and as Members of a Learning Community

Three issues influencing the Life Cycle of the Career Teacher model were described in the first chapter and elaborated in the phase-specific chapters. We underscore what we can *do* collaboratively to incorporate these influences positively in the process of helping teachers grow across the career.

Recognize That Teachers Are Developing Adults

In the teaching profession, as in others, there is a tacit assumption that what happens at home and what happens at work are distinct and always separable events. In reality, life comes to school, and its incumbent stresses and accomplishments are part of the fabric of the learning community. School counselors may have a role to play in facilitating the development of adults as well as students in their schools. Teachers and their professional and paraprofessional adult colleagues may have a role to play in creating support groups, perhaps phase specific, to support growth in the school.

School communities may also be particularly adept in identifying and addressing teacher withdrawal before it becomes persistent and less amenable to intervention. Though everyone has periods of time when he or she may be less engaged in work than others, teachers expressing the initial signs of withdrawal may be assisted if action—professional-development activities, mentoring or teacher-support opportunities, or alternate assignments—is taken early in the process.

Make Schools Successful Developmental Laboratories

A major implication of the Life Cycle of the Career Teacher model is the benefit of staffing a school across the developmental phases. A building in which apprentice teachers are mentored by professional teachers, professional teachers are encouraged to attain the status of expert teachers, and novice teachers are provided with a view of growth across the career can contribute meaningfully to maintaining a healthy, vital learning environment. The presence of an array of persons working in various phases is, of course, not by itself sufficient to encourage professional development. Making explicit linkages across phases—through the provision of well-designed mentoring and coaching programs, the encouragement of teachers to reach new levels of development, the acknowledgment and celebration of phase-related achievements, and the provision of various phase-specific professional-development activities—would better facilitate growth. Similarly, adaptations in workload and differentiated expectations and evaluation systems would also be consistent with viewing schools from a career life-cycle perspective.

Use Conflict as a Means of Encouraging Growth

Rather than viewing conflict as necessarily destructive in a learning community, a developmental view encourages looking at conflict as a means of propelling growth—because it can encourage and support the identification and addressing of problems and concerns. Experiencing conflict with one's own point of view is often an indicator of a transition between phases. The professional teacher and the expert teacher may not view a situation in the same way; in the process of discussing the alternative perspectives, the professional teacher may begin to attain a new level of development. Discussing different viewpoints before moving to solutions can be a useful means of helping people make transitions to new ways of thinking and acting.

Focusing on Social Context as a Force Influencing Teacher Development

The contexts in which we live and work and the situations in which we find ourselves also play an integral role in determining the kind of person and professional we become and how we function in our various roles. Social context is a powerful variable influencing teacher development within the Life Cycle of the Career Teacher model. Here, too, three issues are especially significant to consider, because they are always at work in schools.

Coping With the Constant of Change

Schools are demanding and often ambiguous workplaces. Frequently, expectations for teacher knowledge and skills are revised; often, support for teachers reaching new levels of expectation is not provided in a timely manner. Through preservice programs and professional development across the phases, we must provide means to assist teachers in coping with changes in the workplace and levels of expectation. As we have seen, distinguished teachers often describe themselves as "resilient," able to cope with new demands. In recent years, we have learned a great deal about resilience in children that might apply to developing resilience in teachers. Provision of supportive relationships is a critical element in the development of resilience. Similarly, providing for teachers leads to better decisions about curricula, programs, school climate, and other anticipated changes and has the benefit of improving coping strategies.

Building School Cultures That Work

We strongly advocate the application of the Life Cycle of the Career Teacher model as a framework for school improvement. Issues of structure, workload, climate, curriculum, and interpersonal interactions may all be viewed from within the context of the developmental phases of this model. Opportunities for contextual, phase-related growth must be provided in schools as a means of building cultures that facilitate learning for all members of the community.

Synthesizing External and Internal Societal Forces

It is not only the culture or climate of the local context that influences teacher growth. State policies on licensure and recertification; increasing national expectations for teacher performance and student achievement; movements such as school vouchers; and coping with societal influences such as violence, religion, and drugs all influence the nature of schooling and teaching. School partnerships with universities and local community agencies may reduce gaps between internal and external forces, encouraging collaboration as a means of addressing concerns.

Weaving Threads of Continuity Into the Teaching Tapestry

Though each progressive phase of the Life Cycle of the Career Teacher model is distinct and unique, each also builds upon those that precede it and provides a foundation for those that follow. Continuity among the phases, though, is not limited to their sequential relationship to one another. Each phase is bound by a shared vision of excellence and the articulation of factors that support growth.

A Shared Vision of Excellence

At each progressive phase of this model, teachers continue to develop as competent, caring, and qualified professionals. The definition of those characteristics evolves and changes with each subsequent phase. The following are 3 ways of ensuring that a shared vision of excellence and a respect for differences in phases and persons will characterize the teaching career.

Identifying Standards of Excellence Across the Career and Implementing Means to Assist Teachers in Attaining Them

The National Commission on Teaching and America's Future (NCTAF, 1996) is an example of a standards-based approach to encouraging teacher development across the phases of the career. By specifying standards for teachers to meet at different points in the career, NCTAF has acknowledged and suggested means to address the need for a developmental career path for teachers. For example, institutions engaged in teacher education at the novice teacher phase may meet standards of excellence through attainment of accreditation by the National Council on Accreditation of Teacher Education. Standards for individual teachers at the apprentice teacher phase may be assessed through the Interstate New Teacher Assessment and Support Consortium. Standards for the expert teacher phase may be reached through certification by the National Board for Professional Teaching Standards (NBPTS, 1994).

Creating School Sites to Promote Continual Growth

The Professional Development School (PDS) movement focuses on changing schools to become learning communities that benefit the development and learning of all its members. By combining the resources of teachers, teacher educators, administrators in both schools and universities, and other community partners, PDS sites attempt to address directly and systematically the issues of preservice preparation, ongoing staff development, and school reform.

Relying on an Overarching Commitment to Teacher Development and Making It Context Specific

The Life Cycle of the Career Teacher model makes teacher development the central focus of improving the profession. In this way, it becomes inclusive of the other approaches and provides a means to facilitate teacher growth in the service of student learning and development. Attending explicitly to the central issues of each phase can help us design effective teacher preparation and professional-development programs, create school environments that address the needs of teachers and students, and provide opportunities and time to facilitate growth in each phase, thereby retaining a vital, active, enthusiastic teaching corps.

Factors Supporting Growth

Each phase of the Life Cycle of the Career Teacher model has specific factors that sustain and encourage growth. Across phases, two of those factors are the need to discourage withdrawal and the provision of professional-development activities that promote movement from phase to phase.

The most significant means of responding to factors that impede growth or lead to withdrawal is to recognize their existence across phases and within the profession. Acknowledging and addressing phase-related sources of withdrawal is critical if we are to stem the departure of promising teachers from the profession and maintain vitality across the career among those who remain. Initial withdrawal is easier to address than deep or persistent withdrawal. Acknowledging the existence of withdrawal and recognizing signs of its existence are vital components of a professional-development program based on the life-cycle model. Similarly, having programs and activities available as interventions may be the best assistance in stemming teacher disengagement and withdrawal.

As has been articulated in preceding chapters, concerns exist at each phase that can operate against the continual application of the reflection-and-renewal process. Recommendations for professional-development activities and practices designed to support continued growth are presented in the appendix following this chapter, on pages 119–125.

To sustain growth across the continuum of practice, we must acknowledge and celebrate the achievements that mark personal and professional development within and among the phases of the Life Cycle of the Career Teacher model. For example, novice teachers typically enter the profession idealistically but with little confidence. Thus, celebrating successes and building on them may propel them to the next phase.

Relationships Influencing the Application of the Life Cycle of the Career Teacher Model

Though the reflection-and-renewal process of individual teachers operates as the mechanism to encourage growth in the life-cycle model, that process does not and cannot exist independent of other people. Reflection and renewal may be personal, but the environment that encourages it is interpersonal.

Key Relationships

Strong interpersonal relationships are vital to professional development. The key relationships to consider in applying the Life Cycle of the Career Teacher model are those between teachers and students, teachers and their colleagues, teachers and teacher educators, and teachers and administrators.

The central relationship in the teaching/learning process, and the one addressed most frequently and fully in literature on teaching, learning, and schooling, naturally, is the relationship between teachers and students. From a life-cycle perspective, though, there are rarely discussed points of intersection between student development and teacher development that may influence student learning and development positively or negatively. An apprentice teacher with high expectations for immediate success may experience particular difficulty in maintaining his or her commitment to the profession when teaching an especially large class, encountering a group with extremely diverse learning needs, or working in a school that lacks a peer-mentoring program or provides insufficient administrative support. A professional teacher experiencing initial withdrawal because he or she perceives insufficient growth opportunities may be particularly ineffective when challenged by young people engaged in identity formation.

Collegial support and involvement among teachers offer, perhaps, the most significant influence on whether the reflection-and-renewal process becomes internalized. Teachers in the same phase of development serve as models and a needed support system for one another, providing a network for discussing achievements and concerns characterizing the phase. This interaction must be encouraged from the beginning of preservice education and throughout the career. Relationships among teachers across phases enable mentoring, support, and a vision of future possibilities to be provided for teachers as they develop through the phases, constituting a major argument for ensuring that schools are staffed with teachers at multiple levels of development. Furthermore, an important strategy for nurturing teacher leadership as a means both of enhancing schools and keeping excellent teachers in classrooms derives from the Life Cycle of the Career Teacher model and its emphasis on differentiation of roles over time. The model provides a framework for assisting teachers to make the transition from professional to expert and from expert to the distinguished phase. With each of these transitions, teachers assume additional leadership responsibilities within their buildings and for the advancement of the profession.

As those predominantly responsible for offering initial teacher-preparation programs, ongoing professional-development coursework, and advanced degrees, teacher educators have a special opportunity and responsibility to consider and address the issues associated with each of the phases and with modeling and reinforcing the reflection-and-renewal process in their work. The life-cycle model suggests that teacher preparation and development programs should give novice teachers a strong foundation in the realities of the complex task they have chosen to undertake as teachers; assist apprentice teachers in navigating the transition from student of teaching to teacher of students; support professional teachers in maintaining the expertise needed to grow; provide expert teachers with the means to attain NBPTS certification; encourage distinguished teachers to develop new roles in teacher education and leadership; and invite emeritus teachers to help design, offer, and evaluate teacher education programs and initiatives.

Increasingly, teachers are being held accountable for what students know and know how to do. Teacher educators have an obligation, in this context and working with others, to support teachers in meeting local, state, and national performance standards by offering programs that focus on outcomes over inputs. Finally, in their work in schools—especially in PDS sites—teachers and teacher educators must together redefine their relationship as one based on mutual respect and interdependence and reassess their roles as being collaborative, collegial professionals engaged in the process of teacher education across the career.

The teacher-administrator relationship is critical for determining whether the reflection-and-renewal process and the systematic, forward-moving process of development through phases will be encouraged or impeded in the school. At each phase, administrators have opportunities and responsibilities to address phase-specific needs, provide support and acknowledgement for movement from phase to phase, and intervene in cases of withdrawal. In hiring and inducting new teachers into the profession, the school administrator must assume a major responsibility. Assuming responsibility for the next generation by opening the school to a partnership in the preparation of preservice teachers is one way administrators can support development and, also, provide opportunities for the school to identify prospective candidates for positions. Professional teachers, the competent, dependable backbone of the profession, require support from administrators to maintain their effectiveness and make the transition to expert. Often taken for granted because they cause little trouble, professional teachers may be vulnerable to withdrawal unless their contributions are valued and acknowledged and they are provided with phase-appropriate professional-development activities to ensure their continued growth. Expert teachers may challenge an administrator's traditional view of his or her role; however, shared decision making and leadership are needed to maintain the vitality of the school. Administrators also must be given opportunities to reflect and grow. Administrative-preparation programs must inculcate an understanding of teacher development and how to support it. These programs also must provide support for administrators in a changing environment.

Creating Learning Communities

Though there has been much discussion lately about the importance of creating schools as communities of learners (Lave & Wenger, 1991; Palincsar, Magnusson, Marano, Ford, & Brown, 1998), little attention has been given to strategies for structuring and advancing this concept developmentally. One of the most significant implications of the Life Cycle of the Career Teacher model lies in this area. If strong, supportive, collegial relationships promote the reflection-and-renewal process to encourage and propel movement across the phases of the teaching life cycle, then we must recognize the centrality of school relationships and work directly to assist participants in collaborating effectively over time.

Challenging the Profession to Ensure the Lifelong Growth of Teachers

The outcomes of teaching are reflected in student growth and development. To realize goals for student success, teachers must continually renew and grow with their students. This growth can only occur within a system of support, collaboration, and responsive scheduling.

Access to Support

At all developmental points across the Life Cycle of the Career Teacher model, teachers need support to maintain growth. Beginning teachers adjusting to the demands of a new job in a new culture often have the most difficult assignments in the school. They require access to mentoring programs, support groups, and professional development geared to meeting induction standards. Similarly, professional teachers require acknowledgment of their accomplishments and dependability, support for their assumption of new roles as teacher mentors and leaders, and access to professional-development activities geared to moving them toward the attainment of expert status. Administrators must view the provision of phase-related support as a *right* rather than a privilege for teachers if they are to put the vision of maintaining excellence across the career into practice. Multiple sources of support are also essential; some opportunities for growth can be provided in and by the school, with others emanating from partnerships with universities and communities.

Collaboration and Collegiality

Working together in a mutually supportive environment is the most effective way to ensure development across the career. However, collaboration must be nurtured and taught, beginning in preservice education and continuing over the course of the career. Using the Life Cycle of the Career Teacher model offers a means to promote collaborative interaction among teachers, because it emphasizes the importance of both inter- and intraphase relationships in providing impetus and support for reflection, renewal, and development from novice to expert. Professional-development activities and programs that focus on building teacher leadership and shared decision making are means to support the development and maintenance of collaboration. Partnerships within the school community and between the school and its community, including the higher education community, are also effective strategies for encouraging collaboration.

Time as a Critical Resource

Time is a scarce resource in schools. Yet developing teachers need time to reflect, plan outside the presence of students, and work collaboratively with colleagues in addressing issues of mutual interest. If we wish to implement a vision of excellence for teaching, we must be willing to redesign the use of time in schools to provide for these needs. Planning periods, designated professional-development time during the workday, as well as sabbaticals for teachers who have spent years in the profession and require a period of renewal, are among the ways in which we must redefine time in the teaching profession. Professional-development partnerships can be another important source of time for teachers to reflect and participate in renewal experiences. Innovative programs in these sites may combine teacher education and development programs with support programs. As some innovative partnerships have shown, novice teachers may be given experience in managing a whole classroom while apprentice and professional teachers participate in professional-development programs during the school day. Expert teachers may be the leaders of these programs, working alone or in concert with colleagues from their partner teacher education institution.

Looking to the Future: Benefits of the Life Cycle of the Career Teacher Model

The chapters of this book have unique voices—just like teachers—and still maintain a connection to a shared vision of excellence. The ideas presented in this book provide a framework for viewing the development of teachers and the teaching profession across the career and a mechanism for ensuring that such development takes place for the benefit of teachers and learners everywhere.

Teachers who enter the profession as novices, move through the apprentice and professional phases, and attain the distinction of the expert and distinguished phases are able to maintain excellence for the lifetime of teaching. They embody NCTAF's (1996) vision of great teachers. Furthermore, retired teachers who commit to emeritus activities that move the profession forward have clearly internalized the finest qualities we desire in our teaching corps.

The Life Cycle of the Career Teacher model provides the framework to ensure that *all* students are taught by competent, caring, and qualified teachers. Benefits that result from its application include the following:

- Teachers learn that a teaching career involves continuous growth and a willingness to take steps to ensure their movement toward the expert and distinguished levels.
- Administrators support the reflection-and-renewal process by addressing the needs of teachers operating in the different phases.
- Teachers achieving new phases of development are acknowledged and celebrated.
- The learning environment of the school is changed to a learning community in which students, parents, teachers, and administrators are engaged in a continual learning cycle.
- Teachers in withdrawal are encouraged to reflect on their achievements and current needs and provided with opportunities to grow; teachers who choose not to grow must not be tolerated in the system.
- Teachers entering the profession are mentored, and teachers remaining in the profession receive the administrative and collegial support they need to continue to grow through the subsequent phases of development.

We believe that these many benefits of applying the Life Cycle of the Career Teacher model challenge the profession to take action to implement it as a framework for viewing and addressing proactively the needs of teachers across the continuum of professional practice. The time is right, students deserve no less, and the teaching profession can retain and renew its members, consistent with a vision of excellence across a lifetime of practice.

References

Lave, J., & Wenger, E. (1991). *Situated learning: Legitimate peripheral participation*. Cambridge, England: Cambridge University Press.

National Board for Professional Teaching Standards. (1994). *What teachers should know and be able to do*. Detroit: Author.

National Commission on Teaching and America's Future. (1996). *What matters most: Teaching for America's future.* New York: Author. ERIC ED 395 031

Palincsar, A. S., Magnusson, S. J., Marano, N., Ford, D., & Brown, N. (1998). Designing a community of practice—Principles and practices of the GISML community. *Teaching & Teacher Education, 14*(1), 5–19.

Appendix

Addressing the Unique Needs of Each Phase Through Professional Development: Phase-Related Concerns and Recommended Professional-Development Practices

Novice Teacher Phase

Concern: *Making the transition from student to teacher and school to work.*

Recommendation: Teacher educators must model reflective practices and guide novices through the process of reflection in university coursework by

- Connecting prior experiences and beliefs to new knowledge
- Offering explicit examples of how theory is translated to practice
- Providing instruction and practice in reflective processes—case studies, autobiography, journals

Concern: *Coping with the realities of classroom life.*

Recommendation: Teacher educators/mentors must provide explicit instruction and model the basics of managing a classroom in a variety of internship sites to experience the mechanics of

- Organizing instructional content
- Implementing and maintaining classroom routines
- Assessing and sharing student performance—report cards, portfolios, written narratives

Concern: *Developing instructional skills and behavior-management strategies.*

Recommendation: Teacher educators / mentors must teach novices classroom observation techniques prior to arranging field experiences. This will enable novice teachers to

- Build a professional vocabulary
- Determine cause-and-effect relationships regarding teacher actions and student behavior / achievement
- Evaluate other teachers' instructional planning and delivery and the resulting impact
- Assess their own instructional performance as appropriate

Apprentice Teacher Phase

Concern: *Feeling overwhelmed by full-time responsibilities.*

Recommendation: Teacher educators, mentors, and administrators must offer developmentally sequenced workshops during the year that

- Are timely and offer sufficient information
- Are explicit and include diverse teaching models and specific examples of learning styles
- Accommodate individual needs

Concern: *Feeling a need to be competent and accepted within their school site.*

Recommendation: Prepared mentors offer context-specific information by

- Reviewing district curriculum guides and offering successful methods of delivering content
- Identifying and locating appropriate instructional resources and materials
- Responding to emerging apprentice needs on a daily basis through a team approach

Concern: *Questioning career choice.*
Recommendation: Apprentice teacher cohort groups provide psychological support by

- Identifying common concerns and needs
- Conducting problem-solving meetings and determining appropriate solutions
- Building a sense of community within the school and across the district
- Sharing ideas, materials, and strategies that work

Concern: *Addressing school or district disregard of apprentice teachers.*
Recommendation: Develop schools friendly to new teachers that provide

- Optimum teaching loads for new teachers
- Realistic class / student assignments
- Comprehensive induction programs that continually support new teachers
- Time to confer with and observe other teachers under direction of a trained mentor

Professional Teacher Phase

Concern: *Addressing boredom with the profession and lack of professional growth.*
Recommendation: Because professional teachers must expand and refine their instructional practices, they need professional-development opportunities that

- Support personal reflection—the process endorsed by the National Board for Professional Teaching Standards
- Provide colleagues time and opportunity to learn from one another
- Emerge from their individual professional goals and interests
- Are grounded in current research and best practices

Concern: *Eliminating professional isolation.*
Recommendation: Administrators must recognize the ongoing

contributions teachers make and deliberately design and allow time for teachers to interact, including

- Weekly / daily group-planning time with peers
- Time for peer observations and feedback
- Financial support to attend professional conferences and seminars
- Internet interactions with colleagues

Concern: *Addressing a lack of career growth opportunities.*

Recommendation: In most professions, an ascending ladder of job responsibilities recognizes experience with promotions in title and pay. Because this is not the case with the teaching profession, professional teachers need some recognition of their expanding knowledge and skill, which may be accomplished by encouraging these teachers to engage in

- Peer-coaching teams within a school and district
- Leading on-site in-service workshops
- Developing units of study for school or district sharing
- Coaching preservice teachers in early internships in collaboration with a university

Expert Teacher Phase

Concern: *Finding time for professional growth.*

Recommendation: Expert teachers need time and district support to continue their professional growth, including

- Time to attend professional conferences during and after school
- Encouragement to present at state and national conferences
- Sabbatical leaves to continue their own education

Concern: *Fulfilling a need to share professional talents.*

Recommendation: Administrators and teacher educators must involve expert teachers in preservice instruction and induction programs, including

- Support to create videos of exemplary lessons to share at seminars

- Opportunities to co-instruct methods courses and/or in-service workshops with university faculty members
- Serving as a mentor to novice and/or apprentice teachers in a practicum experience
- Writing for professional journals to share classroom experiences and programs

Concern: *Addressing a lack of career growth opportunities.*

Recommendation: Like professional teachers, expert teachers need some recognition of their expanding, exceptional knowledge and skills, which may be accomplished by encouraging these teachers to

- Coordinate peer-coaching teams within a school or district
- Determine and deliver district in-service workshops
- Develop units of study for district sharing
- Offer input into administrative decisions as site-based team members

Distinguished Teacher Phase

Concern: *Finding time to reflect and opportunities to learn.*

Recommendation: Because distinguished teachers need time and district support to continue their professional growth, school districts should encourage them to

- Attend conferences, both as an attendee and as a presenter
- Assume leadership roles in national organizations
- Present workshops or papers at national conferences
- Take sabbatical leaves to continue their education

Concern: *Fulfilling a need to share professional talents.*

Recommendation: Administrators and teacher educators must involve distinguished teachers in the development and delivery of

- University coursework for novice and apprentice teachers
- Master's-level coursework for professional teachers
- Videos of exemplary lessons to share with the profession
- Methods courses and/or in-service workshops for teachers at various levels of development

- Mentoring activities for novice and/or apprentice teachers
- Writing for professional journals

Concern: *Providing increased professional challenges*

Recommendation: Distinguished teachers need new challenges to fuel their reflection-and-renewal process, which may be accomplished by encouraging these teachers to

- Teach at a new level within the school or district
- Teach a high-risk student group, if appropriate
- Review national curriculum standards for the district
- Serve as consultants to legislative bodies on educational or youth-related issues

Emeritus Teacher Phase

Concern: *Finding opportunities to contribute.*

Recommendation: Emeritus teachers may be offered numerous ways to contribute to the public school system, including

- Tutoring at-risk children in one-to-one relationships
- Mentoring apprentice teachers
- Serving as substitute teachers
- Serving as members of their school boards
- Volunteering as literacy teachers

Concern: *Managing new roles and responsibilities.*

Recommendation: Administrators and teacher educators can engage emeritus teachers in

- Development and delivery of seminars for novice and apprentice teachers
- Delivery of master's-level work for professional teachers
- Supervision of novice teachers
- Opportunities to offer in-service workshops for school staff members
- Service as mentors to apprentice teachers

Concern: *Providing new and different professional challenges.*

Recommendation: Emeritus teachers are in a position to advocate for the teaching profession and should be encouraged to

- Lobby state and national legislatures on educational and youth-related issues
- Serve on advisory councils for local school districts
- Serve as officers on state and national educational associations
- Serve as consultants to legislative bodies on educational and youth-related issues

Index

Note: Page numbers in **boldface** indicate a chart, diagram, or figure.

G

I

L

M

N

P

R

S

T

W

Kappa Delta Pi, International Honor Society in Education, was founded in 1911. Dedicated to scholarship and excellence in education, the Society promotes among its intergenerational membership of educators the development and dissemination of worthy educational ideas and practices, enhances the continuous growth and leadership of its diverse membership, fosters inquiry and reflection of significant educational issues, and maintains a high degree of professional fellowship.

Key to the fulfillment of the mission is the Society's publications program. Kappa Delta Pi's journals, newsletters, books, and booklets address a wide range of issues of interest to educators at all stages of the profession.

Other titles available from Kappa Delta Pi Publications

Star Principals Serving Children in Poverty, by Martin Haberman (1999) — $12.00 M; $18 NM

Star Teachers of Children in Poverty, by Martin Haberman (1995) — $8.00 M; $15 NM

Experience and Education: The 60th Anniversary Edition, by John Dewey (1998) — $20.00 M; $26 NM (cloth) / $12.00 M; $18 NM (paper)

Teacher Leaders: Making a Difference in Schools, by Nathalie Gehrke and Nancy Sue Romerdahl (1997) — $13.00 M; $20 NM

Substitute Teaching: Planning for Success, edited by Elizabeth S. Manera (1996) — $15.00 M; $20 NM

A.C.T.: All Can Thrive—Supporting Mainstreamed Students, by Marjorie Goldstein and Susan Kuveke (1996) — $8.00 M; $15 NM

At the Essence of Learning: Multicultural Education, by Geneva Gay (1994) — $8.00 M; $15 NM

On Being a Teacher, by Nathalie Gehrke (1987) — $8.00 M; $9.75 NM

To place an order, call 1-800-284-3167, or visit KDP On-line at *www.kdp.org*. Quantity discounts are available, and shipping and handling charges will be applied.

M = KDP Member price
NM = Nonmember price

The Corwin Press logo — a raven striding across an open book— represents the happy union of courage and learning. We are a professional-level publisher of books and journals for K–12 educators, and we are committed to creating and providing resources that embody these qualities. Corwin's motto is "Success for All Learners."